Bible Curriculum
TEACHER'S GUIDE

This Teacher's Guide book is meant to be used in conjunction with the Student's Book and the two Coloring/Activity Books.

Copyright 2016 iCharacter Limited. All rights reserved.

Introduction

A Bible curriculum for family devotions or Sunday School, filled with play, art projects, lessons and more to help children learn to apply God's Word.

This curriculum is based on the "Big Bible - little me" book available at www.icharacter.org, Amazon.com and bookstores.

Each lesson includes the following:

Title:
The title refers to the "Big Bible - little me" storybook. It also includes a story number to easily find the related craft pages in the Student's Book.

Reference:
You will find Bible verse references to easily locate the stories in your preferred Bible version.

Topic:
Each Bible story brings out a particular lesson, either a moral character trait or a foundation of faith. It can be helpful when you need an activity to accompany a lesson topic.

A verse:
A Bible verse related to the lesson of the story. Give children something they can take home, add to their craft project or memorize together. These verses are often reworded in order to simplify them for children.

Tell the story idea:
These ideas help children visualize and remember the story. You can use pictures from our Bible or another picture Bible. Ideas for toys and everyday objects/materials that you can use help to bring stories to life and keep children interested.

Games:

These game ideas add variety and give children a chance to get up and move around. Games will be either related to the story or a moral character trait. Very little preparation is needed for these games.

Discussion questions:

After each game, you will find some discussion questions, which offer:

1. An opportunity to calm the children down.
2. Suggestions on how to conclude the story lesson.
3. An opportunity for children to express themselves.
4. A way to help them apply the lesson to their own lives.

Crafts:

Illustrated examples from the Student' Book are listed here. We highly recommend using thick paper in order for the activities and games to work as intended. These arts and crafts are simple enough for most children to do with little help from the teacher/parent. Wide gray lines around the pictures help children know where to cut. Dotted lines are for folding.

Activity Sheets:

All the activity sheets listed here are found in the "Big Bible - Little Me Coloring/Activity Book" available at www.icharacter.org and Amazon.com

Prayer/Praise idea:

Includes ideas for each lesson where children can experience a time of prayer or praise and learning new ways to commune with God. From calm to energetic prayer ideas; your children will find prayer times fun and engaging.

Supplies needed:

Supplies you may need for the activities are listed with each game or craft project. We suggest taking some time to review the content and material beforehand, in order to gather them beforehand.

Old Testament Stories

Story 1: God Makes the World (Creation) .... *Diligence* 1
Story 2: The First Sin (Adam and Eve) .... *Self-control* 3
Story 3: Following God (Noah's Ark) .... *Obedience* 5
Story 4: The Tall Tower (Babel) .... *Humility* 7
Story 5: Abraham Relies on God .... *Dependance on God* 9
Story 6: Waiting for a Baby (Abraham and Sarah) .... *Patience* 11
Story 7: A Wife for Isaac (Rebekah) .... *Initiative* 13
Story 8: Jacob Cheats (Jacob and Esau) .... *Honesty* 15
Story 9: A Special Dream (Jacob) .... *Encouragement* 17
Story 10: A Colorful Coat (Joseph) .... *Comparing* 19
Story 11: A Helpful Sister (Myriam) .... *Responsibility* 21
Story 12: Crossing the Sea (Moses) .... *Confidence* 23
Story 13: God's Ten Commandments (Moses) .... *Justice* 25
Story 14: A Noisy Battle (Joshua) .... *Willingness* 27
Story 15: A Woman Goes to Battle (Deborah) .... *Service* 29
Story 16: A Crazy Idea (Gideon) .... *Flexibility* 31
Story 17: The Strongest Man Ever (Samson) .... *Decisions* 33
Story 18: Gathering Wheat (Ruth) .... *Faithfulness* 35
Story 19: Praises to God (Hannah) .... *Praise* 37
Story 20: Take Time to Listen (Samuel) .... *Attentiveness* 39
Story 21: A Shepherd Boy (David) .... *Caring* 41
Story 22: Facing a Giant (David and Goliath) .... *Courage* 43
Story 23: Songs to God (Kind David) .... *Devotion* 45
Story 24: A Very Wise King (Solomon) .... *Wisdom* 47
Story 25: A Temple for God (Solomon) .... *Worship* 49
Story 26: The Feeding Birds (Elijah) .... *Endurance* 51
Story 27: A Widow in Need (Elijah) .... *Unselfishness* 53
Story 28: Seven Baths (Naaman) .... *Determination* 55
Story 29: A Wee Little King (Joash) .... *Teamwork* 57
Story 30: Three Brave Men (Fiery Furnace) .... *Conviction* 59
Story 31: Surrounded by Lions (Daniel) .... *Peer-pressure* 61
Story 32: Rebuilding the Walls (Nehemiah) .... *Perseverance* 63
Story 33: Queenly Beauty (Esther) .... *Beauty* 65
Story 34: Into the Fish's Belly (Jonah) .... *Availability* 67

New Testament Stories

Story 35: The King is Born .... *God's love* 69
Story 36: Kingly Gifts (Wisemen) .... *Admiration* 71
Story 37: At the Temple .... *God's word* 73
Story 38: Talk about Jesus (John the Baptist) ... *Boldness* 75
Story 39: Jesus picks His Disciples .... *Following Jesus* .. 77
Story 40: Hanging Out With Jesus .... *Kindness* 79
Story 41: Water to Wine Miracle .... *Cheerfulness* 81
Story 42: Jesus Calms the Storm .... *Gentleness* 83
Story 43: Doctor Jesus (Little Girl Back to life) ... *Faith* 85
Story 44: Is That a Bird? (Blind Man Healed) ..... *Asking God* 87
Story 45: Lost and Found (Parable of Lost Sheep) ... *Being responsive* ... 89
Story 46: Friends help out (The Paralyzed Man) ... *Friendship* 91
Story 47: A Boy Shares his Lunch .... *Sharing* 93
Story 48: Stop and Listen (Mary and Martha) .... *Jesus first* 95
Story 49: A Wounded Traveller (Good Samaritan) ... *Compassion* 97
Story 50: The Party Boy (Prodigal Son) .... *Forgiveness* 99
Story 51: A Thankful Return .... *Gratefulness* 101
Story 52: A Changed Man (Zacchaeus) .... *Repentance* 103
Story 53: Into Jerusalem .... *Enthusiasm* 105
Story 54: Not Just a Snack (Communion) .... *Communion* 107
Story 55: Jesus on the Cross .... *Salvation* 109
Story 56: He is Risen .... *Easter* 111
Story 57: Jesus Goes to Heaven .... *Hopefulness* 113
Story 58: Flames of Fire (Holy Spirit) .... *Holy spirit* 115
Story 59: Good News to All .... *Witnessing* 117
Story 60: Heaven to Come (John's Visions) ...... *Heaven* 119

(Story 1)

God Makes the World

(Genesis 1:1) Lesson topic: DILIGENCE

A verse to remember:

"Diligent hands that work hard, make you rich." (Proverbs 10:4)

Tell the story idea:

Gather different colors of play dough and pass them out to each child. As you tell the story, ask the children to create different objects, animals or people, depending on the colors of play dough that they have. Then you can use them as visual aids while you teach your lesson.

Game 1: Creation Guess-Bag

Fill a bag with plastic toys or real objects of things that God has made. Children take a turn to feel inside and guess one object. The child can then pull it out of the bag to show everyone and see if they got right. A few ideas of things to add to your bag: rock, flower, nut, fruit, carrot, leaf, small tree branch, toy animals, or anything that can be identified by feeling.

Game 2: God made me

Each child gets a turn to say "God made me and I start with the letter G (or whatever letter they choose.)" The other children must guess what they are, grass, gorilla, goat? The person who guessed correctly is it. Keep going till all the children have had a turn.

Discussion:

- Can you name all the things that God created? Why or why not?
- Name three of your favorite things that God created?
- Have you ever made something on your own that you were proud of? What was it?
- Isn't God's creation wonderful to enjoy? When do you enjoy it the most?
- Have you ever done something to help out at home that you wanted your mom and dad to know about? (You made your bed on your own. You served yourself breakfast. You put your dish in the dishwasher. You brushed your own hair, etc.)
- How did it feel to accomplish it?

my notes

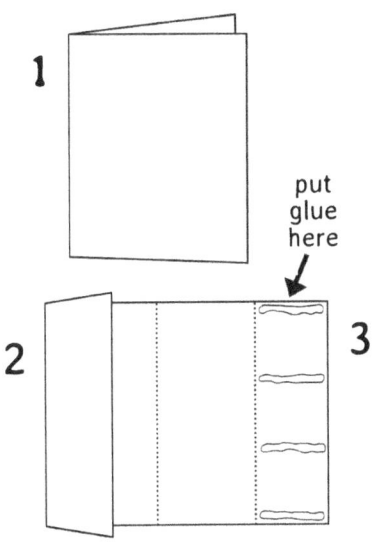

Craft: Creation paper pockets

(See Student's Book)

Give each child an sheet of colored paper. Fold it in half (1). Open it again and then fold both ends halfway to the middle (2). Glue the sides together, as well as the middle for the inside pockets (3). Children cut out and glue the number cards, one onto each pocket (4). Color and cut out all the pictures to place into the appropriate pockets. Again, fold the paper in the middle and place it as a stand-up card (5). This is a great project to help children review the 6 stages of creation.

Activity Sheets:

(See Coloring & Activity Book)

Story color page
Hidden message

Prayer/Praise idea:

Start out with a round of praises, each child thanking God for one of their favorite things He's created. Then have another round for each one to pray for more diligence with something they're learning to do. For example: "God, please give me diligence as I practice wiping the table, or tying my shoes," etc.

(Story 2)

A Sad Mistake

(Genesis 3:6) Lesson topic: SELF-CONTROL

A verse to remember:

"Above all things, guard your heart." (Proverbs 4:23)

Tell the story idea:

Begin by putting out some plates filled with nuts, dried fruits or cookies, onto the table in front of the children. Explain that you're going to practice self-control by having them in easy reach, but they won't get to enjoy them until the end of the lesson. It's great to set goals for kids. This is a very real and tangible picture for them of what self-control looks like.

Another prop to add as you tell the story is a piece of fruit. When Adam and Eve take the bite, have all the kids get a bite of the fruit, or cut up a little piece for each one.

Game 1: City Walls

Read the verse: "Like a city whose walls are broken down, so is a man who doesn't have self-control." (Proverbs 25:28). Talk about this verse by explaining how cities used to need walls for protection (look through books that have pictures of castles and high walls.) If the walls were broken down it meant that the city was in danger. In the same way, if we lack self-control, we are putting ourselves in danger.

Try this activity if your group is not to large: The children can build a big wall made of shoe boxes or plastic containers, lots of books, pillows, chairs or whatever you have available. After the wall is built, pretend to be the bad guy trying to get into the city. Tell them that since they have self-control they are protected. Then you can let the children knock down the wall. Once the wall is knocked down, enter their "city" and "attack" them with tickles.

Discussion:

- How can you be in danger without self-control?
- What makes you and keeps you strong?
- When is it most difficult to practice self control?

Game 2: Temptation Charades

Write various temptations on pieces of paper, such as being sassy, watching the wrong TV show, eating a cookie when told not to, cheating on schoolwork etc. Place all the papers in a basket and have the children take turns to pull one out and act it out for the other children to guess. If the "temptation" is guessed, then the child doing the pantomime will say loudly "Say no to temptation!" Then the child who guessed it takes the next turn.

Discussion:

(for after lesson, while you enjoy the goodies on the table)
- What helped you to resist temptation or control yourselves?
- What can you do to keep away from doing something wrong? (Some examples: look away, recognize that it's a temptation, claiming 1 Corinthians 10:13, distract yourself, walk away, make a plan to avoid the temptation, sing a song, count to 100, picture yourself resisting, set a time goal (For example: we will enjoy this AFTER our lesson, or set a timer, etc.)

Craft 1: A snake chain

(See Student's Book)

Use sheets of green and yellow color paper and cut 6 strips for each child, (3 per color). On each strip of paper, the children can write one word of the following verse: "Above all things, guard your heart." (Proverbs 4:23) Tape, glue, or staple together the far ends of each paper strip as you thread the rings into a paper chain. Alternate the colors. See example. Use some plastic googly eyes and red color paper for the tongue.

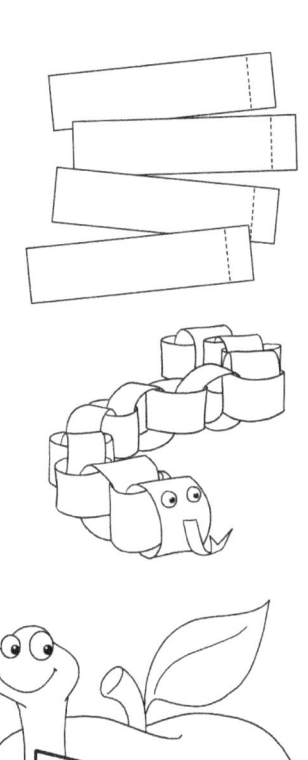

Craft 2: Fruit door

(See Student's Book)

Use the apple image and have each child color and cut out the apple. Cut out the door shape and fold it open on the dotted lines. Then add glue to the back of the flap to paste the door onto the apple. Now, the children can open the door and be reminded of the message from today's lesson.

Activity Sheets:

(See Coloring & Activity Book)

Color page
Trace and Match

Prayer/Praise idea:

(See Student's Book)

Make a tree out of green color paper. Each child gets a little square of red crepe or tissue paper. Normal paper works too. Each child crumbles it up and shapes it into a little ball or fruit. Take turns to ask for God's help in controlling yourself in a specific area, and then glue the fruit onto the tree. The teacher can write the child's name beneath the "fruit", to show that the child has taken a turn.

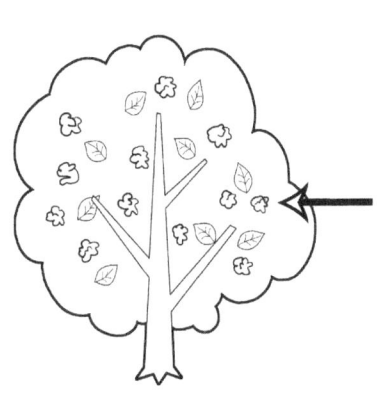

my notes

(Story 3)

Noah Follows God

(Genesis 6:13-22) Lesson topic: OBEDIENCE

A verse to remember:

"Do what is right and good in God's sight." (Deuteronomy 6:18)

Tell the story idea:

Use a big brown box or plastic container along with some toy animals as you tell the story. Use shelled peanuts and little rocks for pretend food to feed the animals, a blue sheet for the water (that you spread over the table) and some white and gray pillows or towels for the children to hold up as the clouds. Have available 7 color papers (or markers or pencils): Red, orange, yellow, green, light blue, dark blue, purple, that a group of kids hold up (one paper each) to make the rainbow.

Game 1: Red light, green light!

The teacher is at one end of the room and kids on the other end. Teacher faces away from the children and gives an instruction related to the story. Each time, the kids take a step forward towards the teacher. When teacher turns around, the children must freeze, or take a step back. Some instructions from the teacher could be: Build a boat, make it big, make it strong, use gopher wood, enough space for your whole family and all the animals, pack up lots of food, stay dry in the boat, send a dove, get some rest, feed the animals, etc. The child to reach to the teacher first gets to be the next leader to call out instructions.

Discussion:

- What can you do when you don't know how to do something on your own?
- Why was it so important for Noah to follow God's instructions?
- Can it be dangerous when we don't obey? How so?
- How could it have been dangerous if Noah didn't follow God's instructions in building the ark?
- Is it always easy to obey your mom or dad or teacher?
- When is it easy to obey?
- When is it difficult to obey?
- How do you feel after you obey?

Game 2: Rainbow change places

Place the chairs in a circle. One child stands inside the circle, while the other children take a seat. The one in the center says, "I see a beautiful rainbow, and in it I see the color ____." The child chooses and says one of the colors of the rainbow, for example "red." Then, everyone sitting down who is wearing something red must quickly changes seat with someone else who is wearing that color. The child in the middle quickly finds himself a seat before someone else sits down. The child without a seat is next to call out a color. Continue until everyone has had a chance to be in the center.

Craft: A Hanging Mobile

(See Student's Book)

Give the children the illustrations to color and cut out. Help them to assemble the pieces together in the right order, as shown in the example. Turn them face down onto the table and tape a string to the back of each picture, from the sun and cloud all the way down to the verse card. Children can take it home and hang it in their rooms.

Activity Sheets:

(See Coloring & Activity Book)

Color page
Find the pair

Prayer/Praise idea:

On a serving tray, place a bunch of plastic play animals, then place it the middle for all the children to have a good look at. Then secretly take one animal off the tray and ask the children to guess which one is missing. Whoever gives the correct answer gets to thank God for that animal and something special that they do or why we enjoy them. For example: a horse gives people rides, a bird sings pretty songs, a cow gives us milk, etc.

(Story 4)

The Very Tall Tower

(Genesis 11:1-9) Lesson topic: HUMILITY

A verse to remember:

God goes against the proud, but gives grace to the humble. (James 4:6)

Tell the story idea:

Use boxes of all different shapes and sizes. During the story, the kids can put them together to build a tall tower. You can also include some tools like plastic hammers, nails and other safe objects to act out with while the people work on the tower. If you have a helper, act out together the part of the confusion of languages. With tools in hands, ask each other for things in a funny or made-up language. Then, act out silly actions, not being able to understand what each other wants. For example, if one asks for the hammer or some bricks the other one may think he's supposed to do jumping jacks or something crazy.

Game 1: Our own weaknesses

Today's activity is a lesson on the benefits of realizing our own weaknesses and the need for help. The activity involves giving the kids a variety of tasks that you know they can't accomplish on their own (some examples might be, lift the table on your own, carry 10 books with one hand, carry your neighbor on your back, hold the box of markers on your head without letting it tip over, do a headstand, etc). After they have a time to at least try the tasks on their own, you can join in to help them accomplish what they wanted to achieve.

Discussion:

- Could you do those things on your own? Why or why not?
- What do you do if you need help? (Ask a friend, parent to help. Pray and ask for God's help.)
- Should we still ask for God's help even if we can do something on our own? Why or why not? (It shows humility and that we are giving God the glory for what we can accomplish)
- What things do you ask God for help with? (Some examples: God, give me strength as I do this project. Lord, give me perseverance as I practice riding my bike. God, I know you made me. I know that with Your help I can feel better today. Please help me with my schoolwork, Jesus, etc.)

Game 2: God blesses the humble

You will need some wooden blocks and Duplo bricks for this activity. Place all the blocks and bricks in the middle of the table or floor. Children take turns to talk about some things they say or do at home or at school or have noticed that other kids do, whether to their brothers and sisters, parents or friends. The rest of the children decide whether it's a humble or a proud remark or action.

If it's something humble and loving, the child lays a Duplo brick for his tower. If it's a proud and bragging thing, they put a wooden block instead. The next child does the same thing and each time the children add to the tower. See what happens to the towers at the end of the round. The children can blow on the towers and see what happens. Next, shake the table or carpet a little and then see what happens.

Discussion:

- Which tower stood strong and firm? And why?
- How did you feel listening to the proud words/actions?
- How did you feel when you heard loving words/actions?
- When you're upset, what is easier to say?
- While in a good mood, do you feel like doing things for others?
- What kinds of words show humility?
- Humility is thinking about whom?

Craft: Babel pop-out card

(See Student's Book)

Give the illustration sheets to each child. They can paint or color the cards and characters, then will probably need a little help to cut the slits on the dotted lines. Follow the example pattern as you fold the slits facing frontward then glue the extra characters onto the walls of the tower, following the example. Now the children can stand up their cards as they review their verse and lesson.

Activity Sheets:

(See Coloring & Activity Book)

Color page
Different languages

Prayer/Praise idea:

Jesus told us a story to show us that there are two ways to pray. Act out the Pharisee with fancy, bright, colorful clothes to attract others to him, head up to the sky, in the middle of the room, on top of the table and shouting so everyone can hear him and see how holy he is. Or show the example of the publican simply dressed, who knew that he was a sinner. With tears in his eyes, he asked God to forgive him for his mistakes. He whispered and told God how sorry he was and how he wanted to please Him. Ask, "Which of these two men were humble before the Lord? Which one do we want to pray like?" All children can kneel down and whisper their prayer to Jesus. First tell Jesus about something they did that was wrong and ask for His forgiveness for. Then each one tells Jesus that they love Him and something that they're thankful to Him for.

my notes

(Story 5)

Abraham Depends on God

(Genesis 11:31-12:9) Lesson topic: DEPENDENCE ON GOD

A verse to remember:

"Show me your ways, dear God, and teach me Your paths." (Psalm 25:4)

Tell the story idea:

Gather some big sheets, strings and pegs. Start the story inside a made-up tent. While reading the part of the story about God telling Abraham to move to another land, have all the children help you undo the tent and carry it to another place. Work together to put the tent back up and then down again for more traveling, till God finally leads Abraham to his new promised home.

Game 1: The blindfold walk

Blindfold a child while the rest of the kids take turns giving him/her instructions of where to go or not go as he makes his way to the other side of the room. "Go one step left, 3 steps forward, a little to the right, now to the left again, etc." Of course, make sure that he doesn't fall or bump into anything dangerous but can get to the other side of the room safely, even between a few fun cushioned obstacles. Once the child has gotten to the other side of the room, change the blindfold to another child. Keep going with as many children who want to do the "blindfold walk".

Discussion:

- How did it feel not being able to see where you were going?
- What worried you the most?
- What gave you trust and confidence?
- Why can we depend on God just like you did with your friends?
- Who knows exactly where you should go?
- Where can we find instructions of how God wants us to live our lives?

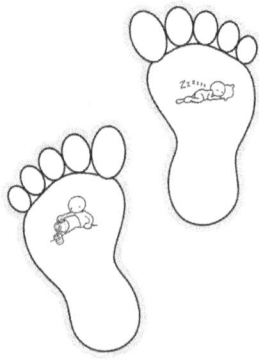

Game 2: Step by step

(See Student's Book)

Help children get into a line, as in a relay race game. Prepare the footprints beforehand and place them randomly on the floor in front of the children standing in a row. The footprints can go around the room or into the hall, and off to another room, as far as you want them to go. Children take turns to step on a footprint and do the actions.

Then they step on to the next footprint and follow that action, all the way till they get to the finish line. Enjoy a special snack or a little chocolate for a job well done.

Discussion:

- Was it easy to follow each step?
- Could you see 5 steps ahead?
- Could you see even 1 step ahead?
- Do your parents always tell you why you need to do something?
- Or do you sometimes have to obey not knowing why?
- Should you obey and follow even when you don't understand?
- What was our blessing and reward for following in this game? How did God bless Abraham for His dependence?

Craft: Travel suitcase

(See Student's Book)

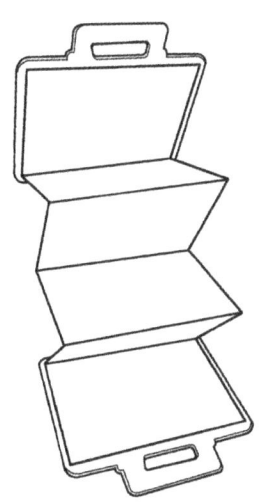

Make a suitcase for Abraham to pack up all his things as he travels to his new home. Color and design the cover of Abraham's suitcase as you wish, then cut each side out. Cut out the other paper illustrations and glue and fold together as an accordion. Now glue each end to the suitcase covers, as shown in example. Children can draw or cut out pictures from old magazines, things that Abraham might have packed to take on his long journey, onto the accordion folded papers.

Activity Sheets:

(See Coloring & Activity Book)

Color page
Help find the way

Prayer/Praise idea: 3 walls

(See Student's Book)

Use the illustrations of the titles made available: Water, land, sky. Tape them to 3 walls in your room. All the children gather to the center of the room and dance, jump, hop or run about. The leader wears a blindfold and gives a signal (clapping twice or blowing a whistle or stopping the music) and all the children must make their way quietly to one of the walls. Then the leader calls out one of the 3 names (Water, land or sky). Whichever children are near that paper, they thank God for something that we depend on, related to it. For example if the children go to "sky" and "sky" gets called out, they could thank God for the clouds because without them we wouldn't have rain. Or for bees, we depend on them to give us sweet honey. Or for airplanes that fly in the sky because they make it possible for us to travel to places far away, etc.

my notes

(Story 6)

Waiting for a Baby

(Genesis 15-17) Lesson topic: PATIENCE

A verse to remember:
"Wait for the Lord. Be strong in heart and be patient for Him." (Psalm 27:14)

Tell the story idea:
Use rods or beans, pencils or blocks or whatever you have available to count out ninety-nine, for children to visualize how old Abraham was when he had baby Isaac and how much patience he must have had to wait so long. Have on hand a baby doll to use as you talk about baby Isaac.

Game 1: Board games
Use this game time to play any simple board game that you have on hand or at home, that will help teach patience while they wait for a turn or for the other children to decide what they want to do on their turn, waiting for when they will win, etc. Playing board games gives loads of opportunity to practice with patience, especially when there are lots of children playing together.

Discussion:
- How did it feel when you had to wait for your turn to come along?
- How many turns did you get? Did it seem like a lot or a few turns?
- How many turns did the other children get? Did it seem like they got more turns than you? Why do you think that is?
- What is the most difficult thing about waiting?
- When is it easy for you to wait for things?
- What things have you seen that other people do while they wait?

Game 2: Countdown chain
Here's an idea that you can do for the next time you're waiting for something; a big event, a birthday, a special day with friends, waiting for the weekend or to go visit grandparents, school vacations, etc. Cut out some strips of paper, could be one color or all different colors, as many strips as there are days to wait for the exciting event. Often times, it's nice to start this as soon as you've told the child about it or as soon as he's aware of it.

On each strip, write down one thing you could do while waiting or something that can make waiting a little easier. It's great to involve the children here and let them come up with some of the ideas as well, as you write them down, one on each strip. Then staple or glue each piece onto the previous one, as a chain and then hang it up. Tell the children that each day they're eagerly waiting something, they can go to the chain, undo a strip and do what it says for that day. Now they'll have something to do as they practice patience as well as doing their countdown to that special day.

Craft: Abraham's tent

(See Student's Book)

Use the tent illustration; cut out on the bolded lines and fold on the dotted lines, as shown in the example. The children can paint or color their pictures, as well as the outside of the tent (opposite side of the paper), making it into any colorful pattern they want. Now as they open the folds, they'll get to retell the story in their own words and be reminded of their new verse on patience.

Activity Sheets:

(See Coloring & Activity Book)

Color page
How old?

Prayer/Praise idea

Explain to the children that God doesn't always answer our prayers the way we expect them to. Sometimes He says yes, sometimes He says no and sometimes He asks us to wait. Pass around the circle, a little toy or stuffed snail, or if you don't have one, just draw or print out a picture of one. When a child has the snail, it's his turn to pray. He can say something like: Jesus, please give me patience while I wait for .... (Each child adds in their own words of what they feel they need to be patient for. Maybe it could be their birthday or a special day or event they're looking forward to, etc.)

my notes

(Story 7)

A wife for Isaac

(Genesis 24) Lesson topic: INITIATIVE

A verse to remember:

Be generous and ready to share. (1 Timothy 6:18)

Tell the story idea:

Use little corks or rocks or pine cones, anything you may have on hand, for the camels and collect as many bottle tops as you possibly can before the lesson. As you're telling the story, ask the helper or one of the children to fill them all up with water, to give all the camels a drink. See what a big job it is and how long it takes. (Interesting fact: camels can drink up to 200 liters in 3 minutes)

Game: Initiative cards

(See Student's Book)

Explain to the children that initiative is responding to a need without being asked. Place the cards face down onto the table. If you want, you can use the blanks to make some of your own. If there aren't enough cards for one or two per child, feel free to make a second copy. Children can answer very differently to the same card. First child picks the top card, turns it around and looks at the picture. He/she must tell everyone how he/she would respond and take initiative in that situation. If they can answer, they get to keep the card till the end of the game. If they don't know, that's okay too. The person next to them can take a guess. There is no right or wrong answer in this game; it depends how each child wants to answer.

Discussion:

- Was there only one particular way to show initiative, or more than one?
- Is showing initiative always doing the same thing for the same person?
- Can you think of someone in your family or of your friends that shows initiative? How do they do that?
- Why does taking initiative and doing things for others make you happy?
- When are you quickest to show initiative? (When you're thinking about helping others or doing things for yourself?)

Activity Sheets:

(See Coloring & Activity Book)

Color page
Who am I?

Craft: Camel Pockets

(See Student's Book)

Create these cute camels using the illustrations provided. You will need 2-4 clothes pegs per child. If you don't have much time, they can do one at Sunday school, and take the other one to do later at home. If you have some students that work quicker than others, they can already work on their second one or help out someone younger than them. Children color and decorate their camels, then glue them back-to-back, leaving a little slit on the top as a pocket. Pinch the pegs onto the camels as the legs. Give each child the verse card and after reading it out together a few times, they can fold it and place it into their camel pocket.

Prayer/Praise idea:

Say something like: "We're going to practice taking initiative with our prayer time today. Whoever has an idea of how to pray, raise your hand!" Then divide up the room into groups or teams of kids. Each one who had an idea of how to pray can help lead their group to praying today.

my notes

(Story 8)

Jacob cheats

(Genesis 25, 27) Lesson topic: TRUSTWORTHY

A verse to remember:

It is required of stewards that they be found trustworthy.
(1 Corinthians 4:2)

Tell the story idea:

Gather some toy people (Play-mobile or Lego) for the 3 male characters in the story. Bring some sunglasses for blind Isaac, along with a tray, a tea-set and some pretend food for the meal that Jacob served.

Game 1: Twin relay race

Play typical relay races with running, hopping, side-walk, etc. but kids have to do it with a partner, while either holding hands or with the ankles tied together with a scarf or some other non-harming material, as you talk about the twins, Jacob and Esau.

Game 2: Truth or Lie?

Tell the children you're going to say something and then they have to let you know whether you're telling the truth or not. For example, throw a ball up in the air, catch it, and say, "I caught the ball." Ask them if that's true. Then rub your tummy and say, "I'm patting my head." Ask again. Then have the next child do an action and say something. It can also be things like, "I'm taller than my dad!" or "I've gone to space!" or "I have a pet rabbit!" etc. things they've done or have, or even descriptions. Each time the other children must say if it's the truth or not. This exercise will help them to distinguish between being honest or lying.

Discussion:

- Was it easy to tell who was telling the truth and who was not? Why or why not?
- How can you often tell when someone is not being truthful?
- Do you always tell the truth? When is it difficult to tell the truth?
- How does it feel after you tell a lie?
- How does it feel after you confess and tell the truth?

Craft 1: Stand-up characters

(See Student's Book)

Use the illustrations of Jacob and Esau to color and cut out. Fold on the dotted lines and stand them up.

Now the children have their cute little characters, all ready to help act out the story.

Craft 2: Attribute wheels

(See Student's Book)

Make these fun little wheels as you learn more about the attributes of Jacob and Esau. Children receive their illustrations, color and cut out the circles. With the help of an adult, they can put in the paper fastener into the middle. Now for a quick review, quiz them on certain attributes, "Who had more hair?" as they use their wheels to find the answers. They will feel so proud of their little works of art to take home.

Activity Sheets:

(See Coloring & Activity Book)

Color page
What did Jacob learn?

Prayer/Praise idea:

Simply make some prayer request cards by drawing little stick figures for non-readers, or write them down for reader students. Before the children come into the classroom or while the children have their heads onto the table with eyes closed and listening to a song, hide them around the room. All the children search for a paper and then sit back down to pray, one at a time, for their request.

my notes

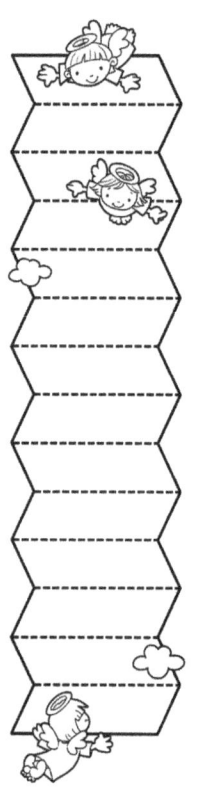

(Story 9)

Jacob's special dream

(Genesis 28:10-22) Lesson topic: ENCOURAGEMENT

A verse to remember:

"It is God who gives me courage and strength and makes my way perfect." (Psalm 18:32)

Tell the story idea:

Use a few Christmas figurines of angels, along with a Duplo or wooden block staircase that you or the children make as you're telling the story. Bring a pillow and blanket to have the children act out Jacob sleeping.

Game: Guess the action

One child starts out by thinking of a loving deed or kind action, something that Jesus would want us to do for others as a way to show encouragement. They act it out while the other children try to guess what they are doing. The person who guesses correctly is the next one to mime a loving deed.

Discussion:

- Is it easy to think of loving things to do for others?
- How do you feel when someone does a loving deed for you?
- What is the best thing that someone did for you, to help make you feel loved?
- What is an encouraging thing that you did for someone else?

Craft: An angel staircase

(See Student's Book)

Use a sheet of yellow or gold paper for each child. Help them to cut it in two, long ways and cut both halves accordion style, then glue them together to make them into a longer staircase. Children can add some glue and glitter or star stickers to make it extra shiny. Color and cut out the angels and clouds figures and glue onto the stairs, as shown on the example. Glue the verse card onto the leftover steps, to help children remember God's encouragement.

Activity Sheets:

(See Coloring & Activity Book)

Color page
Up the stairs

Prayer/Praise idea:

If you're not too far from a stairway, take your prayer time there. All stand in line (two children on each step) and say one word of the prayer each time you take a step up or down. Children repeat the words after you. Or if you're too many to walk up and down the stairs, children can simple sit on the step as they repeat a prayer after you.

my notes

(Story 10)

Josephs colorful coat

(Genesis 37) Lesson topic: COMPARING

A verse to remember:

"Do your very best to live in peace with everyone." (Hebrews 12:14a)

Tell the story idea:

Bring a dress-up box so that each child can pick out something colorful to wear as a pretend colorful coat. If you don't have a dress-up box, you can choose some of your own colorful clothes to put on and off while you're telling the story. Also bring along a set of brown clothes or a brown piece of cloth that you can put on while Joseph is in prison or a slave. Then some fancy clothes to wear while you read about Joseph being the governor of Egypt.

Game: Candy Race

Depending on the space and the amount of children you have, either do this in one shot or divide up into groups and do one group at a time. Place a bowl of nuts or candies on a chair at one end of the room. On the other end, the children line up with a plate next to them. At the "Go!" signal, they run towards the bowl and pick one candy or nut and run back to put it in their plate. During any time the leader can blow his whistle and whoever is not at their plate, gives back the candies they've collected. Start the game as many times as you like.

Discussion:

- Did you feel the game was fair? Why or why not?
- Was it hard to be happy for someone else who got to keep his or her candy, when you didn't?
- Life doesn't seem fair when someone has more than you, but God wants you to be happy with what you have and to trust Him instead of trusting in things to make you happy.
- Before the children leave, distribute all the remaining candies.

Craft: Paper doll

(See Student's Book)

Children color and cut out their Joseph figure. Give them each a toilet paper roll to glue to the back, for support in standing up. If you don't have enough rolls for each child, even half a roll will work.

Then use the coat shape illustration to trace over and cut out from pieces of colorful cloths for the children to glue over their little Joseph figure. Review the verse together before children take it home.

Activity Sheets:

(See Coloring & Activity Book)

Color page
Fashion designer

Prayer/Praise idea:

Thank God for something that your neighbor or friend has that you like but that you don't have. For example, if the girl next to you has pretty clips in her hair and you don't, you can say "Thank You God for Stella's pretty purple clips in her hair, even if I don't have any." Or "Thank You God for Jono's fancy soccer shoes that make him look so handsome." It can even be something other than material things like: "Thank You God that Pete is so good in sports, even though I am not."

my notes

(Story 11)

A Helpful Sister

(Exodus 1:1,2,10) Lesson topic: RESPONSIBILITY

A verse to remember:

"He who is faithful in the little things will also be faithful with much." (Luke 16:10)

Tell the story idea:

Use a blue sheet or cloth to put over the table to use as the "River Nile". Bring a doll, small blanket and basket or container to float over the water. If you have a crocodile stuffed animal, bring it along for extra suspense, ha. Pick some leaves or tall grass to put in front of your face when you're pretending to be the big sister hiding. If you have a little princess crown, bring it for one of the little girls to wear for the princess part.

Game: Responsibility basket

Collect some cut-out pictures from magazines or printed pictures of some items that you use to clean and tidy up around the house, or take care of a baby brother or sister, help cook or garden, etc. Place them in a basket. For older children, the first player picks one of the objects from the basket while the other players ask him questions to try to find out what that object might be. They may ask questions like: Do you use it with another person? Do you use it outside? Does it make noise? Is it a useful object to help you do things? Is it big? Can children and adults use it? The first one to guess what it is, is the next one to pick from the basket. For younger children, an alternative would be just to act out the way to use the object and the others guess what it is.

Discussion:

- What are some items that you like to use most, that help you practice responsibility?
- What are some things that you can use only once you've learned to be responsible? (car, kitchen appliances, tablet, etc.)
- Why can some things only be handled with care and responsibility?
- How did Miriam show that she was a big sister and responsible?
- How would she have acted without responsibility?
- How can you show responsibility when you're with others?
- How are you learning responsibility in your home?

Craft: Basket boat

(See Student's Book)

Make a basket from mini yogurt or pudding cups. Cut out strips of brown paper for the children to glue over the cup so it looks more like a basket. Then each child can add a little piece of cloth inside, to use as the baby's cozy blanket. Children color and cut out their baby Moses illustration and then place him into the cloth. With the other illustrations, paint the grass green and the water blue. Cut them out, then fold and glue the grass in place, as shown on example. Add a little sticky tape or dab of glue to place the basket in place as well.

Activity Sheets:

(See Coloring & Activity Book)

Color page
Find the differences

Prayer/Praise idea:

All the children take their little hand-made baby Moses crafts and rock their baby to sleep as they pray and repeat this prayer after you. "Dear God, thank you for keeping baby Moses safe in the river. Thank you that his little basket didn't tip over. Thank you that the Princess found him and took good care of him. Thank you that You always keep us safe and You take such good care of us. Help us to grow up and learn to take care of ourselves, others and the things around us, too, by learning to be responsible. Amen"

my notes

(Story 12)

Crossing the Red Sea

(Exodus 13-15) Lesson topic: CONFIDENCE

A verse to remember:

"Nothing at all is impossible with God." (Luke 1:37)

Tell the story idea:

A fun way to act out the story is to use two big blue or white sheets and place them in the middle of the room. Pretend to be Moses, pray and lift your hands up as you walk across the room, on "dry land", while half of the children pull the sheets apart, dividing the waters. The other children join Moses through the Red Sea, acting out the people of Israel, and then thanking God for the miracle.

Game: Crossing the Sea

In the middle of the room, place a blue sheet onto the floor as a pretend "Red Sea". Each player is given 2 sheets of brown paper shaped into giant footprints. The player must cross "the Red Sea" stepping only on "the dry footprints" (the sheets of paper). At first the player steps on one of the sheets with his/her feet. He/she places another sheet of paper in front of him/her. Then he/she must step on this sheet and put the previous one in front of him. You can take turns with one or two children at a time, or have all the children doing this at once, if you have enough footprints prepared.

Discussion:

- Was it easy to cross to the other side of the room with your papers?
- What made it easy or difficult?
- Did you know that you were safe doing it? Why or why not?
- What if it was real water, would you still feel safe? What would have happened to the papers?
- What are some things that you might be scared or worried about sometimes?
- Why don't we need to feel worried at all? Who's big footprints can we be secure on?

Craft: Moses and the Red Sea

(Simpler version: See Student's Book)

Color and cut out the illustrations. Then fold Moses upward, so it looks as if he's standing up. If you have, give a few small pebbles to each child to glue onto the ground area as an extra 3D look.

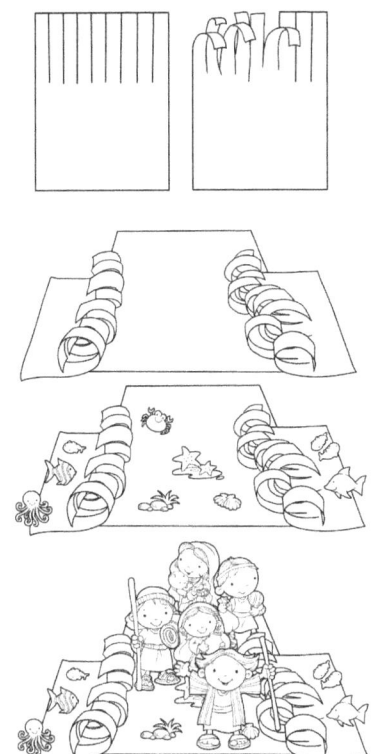

Cut out plenty of thin strips of light and dark blue papers for the children to glue to either sides of the "dry ground" paper, to show the waters parting. If they still have time, they can curl them up with scissors to make them look like waves. Glue the verse card in the middle of the ground area and review it together before leaving.

Craft: Moses and people diorama

(Difficult version: See Student's Book)

For each child, you will need 1 A4 sheet of blue paper and 1 brown paper, also A4 size. For the brown paper, preferably use thicker paper or cardboard from a cardboard box or cereal box, if you have. Cut out slits of the blue paper about a third way down the middle. Then use the blade of scissors to curl each strip upward. Glue the two "Sea" papers onto the piece of brown cardboard leaving a space down the middle. Color and cut out Moses and people illustrations, then fold the flaps behind and glue them onto the middle aisle of the brown paper, in between the waves, making them stand up. Color and cut out the fish and sea creatures and glue them onto the water or land.

Activity Sheets:

(See Coloring & Activity Book)

Color page
Finish drawing

Prayer/Praise idea: Roll the die

Think of 6 prayer requests beforehand, and give them each a number from 1-6. Now use a die and each child takes a turn to roll. Whatever number they land on, they check the list for what they should pray for. It's okay if a few children pray for the same request. Once they pick their request, they can pray for it right away.

(Story 13)

God's Ten Commandments

(Exodus 19,20) Lesson topic: JUSTICE

A verse to remember:

"If you love Me, follow My commandments." (John 14:15)

Tell the story idea:

Use 2 cereal boxes that are gray or brown on the inside. Take them apart and turn them inside out and then glue or tape them back together again. Now, with a thick permanent marker you can write out numbers 1-10 (Roman numerals if you like), 5 numbers on each box. If you have enough space, you can even write out the commandments real simply. This can be used as a visual aid for your lesson.

Game 1: Hangman

On a white board or large sheet of paper, make lines for each letter in the word TEN COMMANDMENTS. Have the alphabet listed on the wall or on cards in the middle of the table for the children to see clearly. They take turns calling out letters to guess the words. Draw a hangman as you go, for each letter that is called that doesn't belong in the words "Ten Commandments".

Discussion:

- Is it easy to remember all of the 10 commandments?
- Which one do you remember best and why?
- Which commandment do you find most difficult to remember to obey?
- Why did God give the 10 commandments?
- Give an example of why rules are for our own good and help to keep us safe?

Game 2: Guessing bag

You will need a cloth bag along with a few objects to go inside it (see below). Begin the game by placing on the table, the 10 commandments sheet, which includes the examples and verses, but leaves out blank boxes for the objects. The children dig into the bag, while closing their eyes, feeling and guessing an object. Once they guess, they can take it out of the bag, show it to everyone and place it on the commandment text that they think fits it best. Read out the verse and explanation before going on to the next child.

10 objects to place in the bag are:

1. Medal of honor (those small ones tied to a string)
2. Purse or wallet with money
3. Toothpaste and a toothbrush

4. Calendar, or scroll or toy church building
5. Picture frame of a Mom and Dad
6. A plastic toy sword or gun, or a little gravestone and cross.
7. A red paper or felt heart with a photo of a bride and groom, that's broken and cut in the middle.
8. A paper cut hand with candy taped on to it.
9. A string with the words "lie, LIE, LIE" (the words written getting bigger and bigger each time) attached to it.
10. A bracelet or jewelry, and a super car mini model.

Craft 1: Ten Commandments Key-chain

(See Student's Book)

You will need a simple key-chain per child. Use the illustration given for the children to color and cut out as they wish. They can make a little drawing in the back of each card to help them remember each commandment. Once they're all finished, punch a hole into each one and put them in order into the key-chain for the children to carry around with them as they learn and practice the 10 Commandments.

Craft 2: Ten Commandments tablets

(See Student's Book)

Children can make their very own tablets of the 10 commandments by using the illustrations provided. Take the little stone tablets, cut them out on the bolded lines and fold over on the dotted ones. Glue the backs of each one onto the scroll page as shown in the example here. Children can color and decorate the little numbers and windows as they wish. Now they get to write or draw something about each commandment, that they remember from the lesson. Review the verse together.

Activity Sheets:

(See Coloring & Activity Book)

Color page
Fill in the blanks

Prayer/Praise idea:

Now use the same "guessing bag" objects for your prayer time. If you don't have enough objects because there are more than 10 children in your class, just put the objects back in the bag once the first 10 children have prayed, for the next round to use. Each child picks one out and prays for something relating to that "Ten Commandment". For example, if one child picks out the picture frame of mom and dad, he can pray something like: "Help me dear God, to obey and respect my mom and dad." or if he has the papers with lies, lies, lies: "Help me to always tell the truth," etc. This is also a good way to review what they have learned in today's lesson.

my notes

(Story 14)

The battle of Jericho

(Joshua 5,6) Lesson topic: WILLINGNESS

A verse to remember:

"If you are willing and obedient, you will be blessed." (Isaiah 1:19)

Tell the story idea:

Use a kitchen towel roll (or an empty juice bottle) as a horn. Have big number cards (1-7) or magnetic numbers to add to your white board or table to show every day they walked around the city, as well as for the last day when they walked the 7 times, and count them out together. To form the walls, you could pretend with big strong books, that you open and stand up in the middle of the table.

Game 1: Simon says

Instead of the typical "Simon says" we will say "Joshua says". All the children line up on one side of the room. The leader is on the other end and calls out "Joshua says..." as he says and shows an action for the children to copy. But beware because as soon as he says and does an action without saying "Joshua says" beforehand, the children should not copy it, or they are out. Keep playing this game until all the kids have gotten the hang of it or till there is one last winner.

Discussion:

- Do we always obey whenever we feel like it?
- Should we obey even when we don't feel like it?
- If someone tells you to do a wrong thing, should you obey? Why or why not?
- Should we obey even when we don't understand the reason for doing it?
- How do we feel after we obey?
- Did someone ever make fun of you for following instructions or obeying your mom or dad?
- What are some blessings from obeying?
- What are some consequences from disobeying?

Game: "I am willing!"

Children sit on the floor with their backs against a wall, as the teacher stands on the other side of the room and calls out different scenarios. If the teacher says something GOOD that the children should do, the children jump up and say "I am willing!" as he takes a small jump forward.

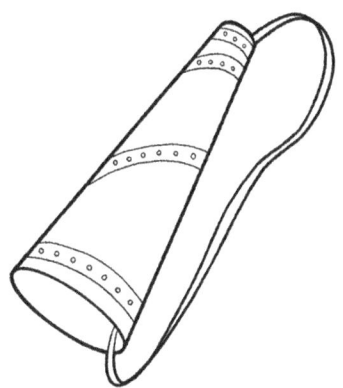

If the teacher says to do something wrong, the children quietly take a scoot backwards, instead. (A few ideas of scenarios the teacher may call out: Go to bed on time; brush your teeth; swear at your friends; stomp your feet when you're angry, read your Bible; make your bed; pray every day; steal some candy; eat cookies when nobody is looking; watch a bad TV show; set the table for your mom; call your Grandma to say hi, cheat on a test at school, etc.)

Craft 1: Joshua's horn

You will need some heavy-duty construction paper or lightweight cardboard, ribbon or yarn and some other decorative elements, sequins, buttons or glitter. Start out by having the children roll their construction paper into a cone shape and fasten it with tape. Trim any edges that stick out so you have a nice even cone. Run a piece of the ribbon or thick yarn through the horn from the tip of the edge and tie it together as a handle. The children can decorate their paper horn as elaborately or as simply as they wish and write the words "God keeps His promises!" somewhere on top.

Craft 2: The walls of Jericho

(See Student's Book)

Have the children build their own little Jericho city, using a rectangular box like an empty milk carton. Children paint the top half of their box blue for the sky, or if it's easier they can glue some blue color paper onto each side. They can add the clouds illustrations and include some puffy cotton on top. Cut out some red or brown rectangle shapes for the bricks and glue them all over the bottom half of the carton, as well as the Joshua character figure, after you've colored it. On the blue/sky part of the box, glue the verse card that says: "Be willing and obedient!"

Activity Sheets:

(See Coloring & Activity Book)

Color page
Into Jericho maze

Prayer/Praise idea: The Jericho shout prayer

Give each child a cup or a jug as you pass out the prayer requests. For example, have the few children on the left side of the room pray for parents and teachers. Those on the right side, pray for children who are learning about God's Word. The children in front can pray for the sick, and the ones in the back pray for protection and safety, etc. When everyone is ready, each team in turn yells out their own prayers, all at once into their cup or jug as loudly as they can. Be ready to hear some mighty "Jericho shout"!

(Story 15)

Deborah goes to battle

(Judges 4-5) Lesson topic: SERVICE

A verse to remember:

"I can do everything through Him who gives me strength." (Philippians 4:13)

Tell the story idea:

All the girls stand up and read today's verse together. Tell the girls to stand up whenever you're talking about Deborah. The boys stand up when it's talking about Barak and the rest of the soldiers. Use a broom as a pretend horse for Deborah riding into battle, and a green umbrella as her pretend "palm tree" that she likes to sit under while she helps her people.

Game: Questions and actions

Use this list of questions about the story, along with the 10 fun actions. Spin a bottle to find out who starts to answer first and then continue to spin for each one's turn. If he answers correctly, the leader gives him an action and he leads everyone to do it together. If he gets it wrong, he has to do the action on his own.

Question ideas (You can include some of your own too):
1. What kind of job did Deborah normally do?
2. What was happening to God's people?
3. Who did God choose to lead the battle?
4. Why did Deborah lead and not a man?
5. Who won the battle?
6. What did God's people do after their victory?
7. What is a judge?
8. When people have problems, who do they go to for help?
9. How do you feel when you serve others?
10. Does God want us to be His servants and help others?
11. What kinds of things can we do to serve others?

Action ideas (You can include some of your own too):

1. Take a partner and while one lies on the floor, the other picks him up. And then do it again switching roles.
2. Do 4 jumping jacks and after each one blow a kiss.
3. Take a partner by the hand and spin around together 5 times
4. Skip on your tiptoes around the room pretending to be a fairy sprinkling love around
5. Pretend you're on a horse, galloping to help someone in need
6. Pretend you're serving someone tea and cookies
7. Pretend you're helping your dad do gardening

8. Pretend you're helping to take care of your baby sibling
9. Pretend you're petting and feeding your pet dog
10. Pretend you're setting the table
11. Pretend you're vacuuming/sweeping the floors to help Mom
12. Go out of the room and then come back in with a smile
13. Go out of the room and then come back in with a funny face
14. Pretend you're a superman flying to go and help someone

Discussion:

- Did you prefer doing the action all together or on your own? Why is that?
- How did you like pretending to do things for others?
- Which of those things have you done for real?
- What other things have you done at home to serve others?
- Who gives you strength and joy in doing things for others?
- Do you feel as strong and happy when you do things for yourself?

Craft: Deborah's Palm tree

(See Student's Book)

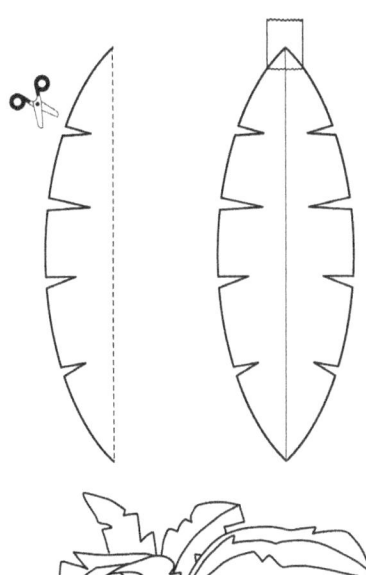

Remind the children how Deborah was a judge and would help counsel people to make wise choices. She would sit under a palm tree and pray and ask for God's strength. Give each child a kitchen paper towel roll (or thick brown paper taped together into a roll shape). They can use a brown marker to draw little lines all over the roll to decorate it to look as the tree trunk. After they color and cut out the Deborah figure, they can glue it on their roll, as shown in the example here. Use the leaf illustration to trace onto green color paper, cut out and fold in half as you cut little leaf slits, see example. Add a piece of tape onto one end of the leaf and place on the inside of the roll. Do the same for all your leaves. Each child will need about 5 leaves per tree. Glue the verse card onto the other side of the tree trunk, opposite Deborah.

Activity Sheets:

(See Coloring & Activity Book)

Color page
True or False

Prayer/Praise idea:

Go around in order of seating arrangements as you pray for something that starts with the same letter as your name. For example, if your name is Mary, use the letter "M", and pray for miracles or mommy, anything that begins with the letter "M", etc.

my notes

(Story 16)

God helps Gideon

(Judges 6-7) Lesson topic: FLEXIBILITY

A verse to remember:

Work hard and cheerfully at whatever you do, as though you were working for the Lord. (Colossians 3:23)

Tell the story idea:

Get a bowl of water and show the kids how the soldiers lapped with their hands. Use a flashlight for the torch that Gideon used (as you close the curtains or shutters for a minute during the reading of the night scene).

Game: Follow the leader

Each child takes a turn to do some action or movement walking around the room, for the other kids to follow. When the whistle blows the next child becomes the leader. Remind the children that what makes a good leader is knowing how to follow. Being able to follow takes flexibility. Being able to adapt to different people, thoughts and styles will benefit your children as they travel through life.

Discussion:

- Was it easy to keep changing the leader?
- When did you follow the leader? When he did something right? Or when he did something wrong?
- What do you do when he does something wrong? What leader do you follow then?
- Do you sometimes think about what you want to do and have a plan for your day?
- Does it usually work out exactly like you expect it to? Why or why not?
- What happens when things and plans change? What can we learn from that?

Craft: Fire torch

(See Big Bible – little me Craft book.)

For each child you will need: a paper towel roll, 3 sheets of felt (or normal paper can do too), red, orange and yellow. You also need three pipe cleaners, red, orange and yellow (1). Cut a slit in the middle of each piece of felt (2), and then put the pipe cleaners through (3) and then twist them at the top. Use a little fabric or wood glue between each layer of felt to keep them in place.

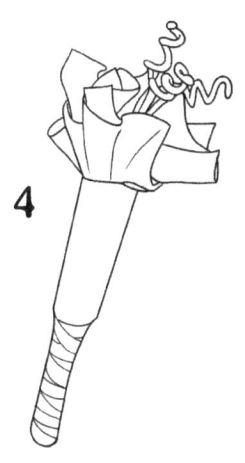

Next, gather them all up on the bottom and stuff them into the paper towel roll which should also be lined up with glue (4). Children finish this project by decorating or painting their torches. Glue the memory verse card onto the torch handle. "Work hard and cheerfully at whatever you do!"

Activity Sheets:

(See Coloring & Activity Book)

Color page
Story words

Prayer/Praise idea: Amen prayer shout

Children can use their torches to pray. Whenever the teacher says something, the children shout out "Amen!" as they hold up their torches. Again the teacher continues with a sentence and again the children shout "Amen!" until the prayer is finished.

(Story 17)

Samson the Strong

(Judges 13, 16) Lesson topic: DECISIONS

A verse to remember:

"If you don't know what to do, ask for God's help, and He will be happy to show you what is right." (James 1:5)

Tell the story idea:

Bring in a big strong man or young person to act out Samson for you. Have him carry a book, then a chair, then a child with just one hand, then let him try to carry you and everyone laughs. If you have a long hair wig (for him to wear), use that too.

Game 1: Three Solutions

Divide up the children into 3 groups. One group calls out "Stop and pray!" the next: "Ask others for help!" and the third group says "Trust God to work it out!"
Think up a list of random questions that you ask the whole group. Each group shouts out their answers together if they think their answer is the right one. There can be more than one answer at once if need be. This game is a good reminder of what to do when you don't know what to do, thus helping to lead to wise choices even in real life.

A few example questions:
1. What do you do if you can't find your sock?
2. What do you when you get stuck with your homework?
3. What if you're sick and can't play with friends for the today?
4. What to do if you don't know which snack to choose?
5. What do you do if you're in bed and can't sleep?
6. What do you do if you're feeling bored?
7. What if you can't reach something that's too high for you?

Discussion:

- How does it feel when you don't know the answer to something?
- How does it feel to know that you always have someone that you can count on to help you?
- Which one of the answers (from the 3 groups) do you remember to do most often? Or which one works the best for you?

Game 2: Dominoes

Let the children line up a set (or more if you have) of dominoes. Once they are all lined up, push down the first one and watch how all the dominoes get knocked down in turn.

Discussion:

- How are dominoes like the choices we make?
- If we make wise choices, are we happy? Are others around us happy?
- What about if we make wrong ones? Who do we hurt?
- Should we ask for God's help in making decisions?
- Who has a story or testimony to share about that?

Craft 1: Decision-making notebook

(See Student's Book)

Use the little book illustration page for each child. Cut out the papers and staple them together. Children can color and decorate their little book covers. Encourage them to take their booklets home and draw about each time they make a good choice about something and the pleasant consequences. Have them bring their little booklets back in a week or two, to share with others how their wise choices went, as you enjoy a special yummy treat together!

Craft 2: Samson wheel

(See Student's Book)

Children color the illustrations. Cut out on the gray lines. The children may need some help to cut inside the top half of the wheel. Use a brad to put the circles together, the cut circle on the top and the heads underneath. Children can retell the story of how Samson was strong when he listened to God and kept his hair long. When he made wrong choices, his hair got cut and he became weak. Glue the verse in the back of the wheel, to review together.

Activity Sheets:

(See Coloring & Activity Book)

Color page
From where?

Prayer/Praise idea:

Three envelopes prayer: Have 3 bowls or envelopes labelled: Thank you! Sorry! Please! Give each child 3 pieces of blank papers for them to draw their requests on. First they draw something that they want to thank God for, then something they are sorry about and lastly something that they would like to ask God for. They put each paper in the appropriate bowls/envelopes. Don't forget to check the envelopes from time to time or in a couple week's time, to let everyone share in the joy of answered prayers.

my notes

(Story 18)

Ruth honors Naomi

(Book of Ruth) Lesson topic: FAITHFULNESS

A verse to remember:

"A faithful man will be filled with blessings." (Proverbs 28:20)

Tell the story idea:

Dress up as Ruth with a dress, scarf, etc., along with some cloth bags as your luggage. Bring a basket of grains of wheat or the wheat plants (if you can find them, or something that looks similar)

Game: Harvesters and Gleaners

(See Student's Book)

Teacher places lots of pieces of grain on the ground. You can use the illustrations provide if you like or simply make your own from yellow colored paper. Put on some music while the children pick up and glean the wheat from around the room. When the music stops the children freeze. Put the music back on and the children get back to gleaning. Continue until all the wheat is collected. Once they finish, you can enjoy a little wheat bread or cake together.

Discussion:

- What if you had to go hunting and searching for your food each day? Would that be a lot of work?
- Do you think you'd get hungry?
- Now what if you only had wheat to eat, for breakfast, lunch and dinner?
- Who gets your food for you? And then who cooks your food?
- Have they ever missed or forgot to cook for you? If not, that means that are very faithful.
- What else do they do for you each day?
- What things are you faithful to do? For yourself? For your parents? For others?
- Do you think others appreciate you when you are faithful?

Craft: Ruth scenery

(See Student's Book)

Have children make the simple stand-up card for Ruth's story by coloring and cutting out the figures and background. Remember to cut on the gray lines and fold on the dotted lines. Now place the figures in place as shown on the example.

Activity Sheets:
(See Coloring & Activity Book)

Color page
Corns of wheat

Prayer/Praise idea: Family circle
(See Student's Book)

A little in advance, cut out a people shape accordion for each child. Each one can write the names of the people in their family, their dad, mom, brother and sister. Then, they can write or draw a little prayer request on each person's cutout, as they pray for them.

my notes

(Story 19)

Hannah thanks God

(1 Samuel 1,2) Lesson topic: PRAISE

A verse to remember:
Be glad and rejoice for surely the Lord has done great things. (Joel 2:21b)

Tell the story idea:
Use a scarf to act out Hannah as you're telling the story. Use a doll for baby Samuel.

Game: Hot potato
You can use either a real potato or a ball or stuffed animal for this game. All children sit in a circle and pass the ball around from person to person. When the music stops or the leader claps his hands, whoever has the ball freezes. The child who has it or touched it last praises God for something.

Discussion:
- Did you like the ball landing on you?
- How does it make you feel when you stop to praise God?
- When do you take time throughout the day to do that?
- Are there certain days or special days that you do it more often? Why and when ?
- When we pray and ask God for something, what does He do ? (He listens and loves to answer with the things that we need and sometimes even with things that we want.)

Craft: Praying hands
(See Student's Book)

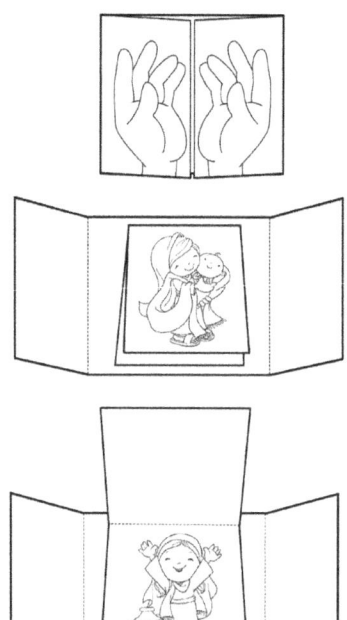

Color the pictures of the hands and Hannah. Cut out the gray lines and fold on the dotted lines so that the hands are on the front, outside of the card. Take a half sheet of A4 paper and fold it once as you glue Hannah with her baby on the front and Hannah praising God on the inside, as shown in the example. Cut off any excess paper so that it fits inside the praying hands. Now the children can retell the story of Hannah praying (using the praying hands), then open the hands and see how God answered her prayer. What did Hannah do next? Open the flap to find out.

Activity Sheets:
(See Coloring & Activity Book)

Color page
Find the same

Prayer/Praise idea: Prayer chain

Give each child in the group a strip of colored paper and encourage them to write or draw something that they're thankful for and would like to praise God for. One at a time, they tell God about it. As each one finishes their turn, fasten their strip of paper onto the previous one. Together, they make a decorative praise chain that you can hang across your classroom to remember all the things they are thankful to God for.

(Story 20)

Samuel listens

(1 Samuel 3: 1-19) Lesson topic: ATTENTIVENESS

A verse to remember:

"I will listen to what God will say to me." (Psalm 85:8a)

Tell the story idea:

Collect little toy animals or objects that make noise, for example: dog, cat, lamb, lion, bird, radio, guitar, drum, blender, remote control, telephone, etc. Throughout your story, show one of the objects and all the children repeat together, "Shhhh, little lamb, it's time to pray!" Or "Shhhhh, little guitar, it's time to pray!" "Shhhhh, little radio, it's time to pray!" etc. to help them visualize that we can also turn ourselves off when it's time to pray and listen to God. Bring a pillow and a blanket to act out Samuel's story.

Game 1: Listen and point

All children sit in their seats with their hands over their eyes. Choose one person to be "it" and have him move from one place to another. He calls out "I'm here!" and all the children, still with their eyes closed point to where they hear him. The first child who points correctly or the closest to the right point is the next caller. Keep playing for as long as the children are having fun and getting the concept of being real quiet in order to listen attentively.

Discussion:

- Was it easy to hear the person calling? Why or why not?
- Who is always with us and loves to talk to us?
- Can we be attentive to listen to Him at any time of the day?
- When is it most difficult to hear Him?
- When is it easiest to listen?

Game 2: Chinese telephone

Children form a circle and one child starts out by whispering something into the next child's ear. He can only say the message once. The other child whispers exactly what he heard to the next child and on it goes down the circle. The last child announces to everyone what he heard. Try again another time and this time add a few noises in the background, some music, shuffling papers, moving chairs, and then ask the children what they heard:

Discussion:

- How were you able to listen and understand when everything was quiet?
- And how did it work when there were extra noises in the room?
- How do you like to hear God's messages to you, clearly or obstructed with noise?

Craft: Listening ears
(See Student's Book)

Use the craft illustration of the big ears. Have the children paint and then cut them out on the gray lines. Now use a colored paper strip, measure onto the child's head, glue the ears on the sides and fasten together with tape. Children can also help each other with this part. Glue the card or write out the verse on the front of the strip of paper and read it together before leaving.

Activity Sheets:

(See Coloring & Activity Book)

Color page
What did Samuel do?

Prayer/Praise idea: Listening practice

Before prayer time, once again include another couple of animals or objects to say shhhhh to, like for during the story. Then repeat together, "Shhhhh, little me, it's time to pray!" All children sit real still and quiet and pray for whatever sounds they hear. A few ideas could be: if you hear a child coughing, pray for his healing. If you hear a bird singing, thank God for the birds. If you hear a baby crying, ask God to help the baby be happy and well cared for. If you hear a clock, ask God to help you stay on time. If you hear a car, ask for God's protection for while you travel, etc.

my notes

(Story 21)

A shepherd boy

(1 Samuel 16) Lesson topic: CARING

A verse to remember:

Whenever you are able, do good to people who need help. (Proverbs 3:27)

Tell the story idea:

Collect some white cotton balls to use as little pretend sheep, a green sheet or cloth for the grass, a thin blue cloth or paper for a stream of water. You can make your own sock puppets or masks for acting out the wild animals. Children love pretend games. Give them a small stick or branch to use as a shepherd's staff as they search out their sheep.

Game 1: Bingo game

(See Student's Book)

Each child has a Psalm 23 bingo board. Feel free to make more copies if needed. Cut out the text cards and sheep beforehand. The teacher picks the first card on his stack and reads out the part of the verse on the card as he shows it to the players. (For older children, you can just read the verse and see if they can guess what picture it belongs to). If a child guesses it right and thinks that it belongs to him, he raises his hand. If he's correct, he gets to place a little sheep card onto the matching picture on his board. The child that fills up his board first is the winner.

Game 2: Hide and listen.

All children hide around the room or garden (if you're playing outdoors for this game), pretending to be little sheep. The child chosen to be the shepherd calls out a name. That child comes running and says, "Here I am, you called me!" being an obedient and listening sheep. Now it's that sheep's turn to the be the shepherd and call out for another sheep who is hiding.

Discussion:

- How does it feel when your sheep come right away?
- How does it feel when they don't listen and obey?
- What if they don't come right away because they are in danger and need help?
- What would you do if your sheep was in danger?
- How do others care for you when you're sick or in need of help?

Crafts: A Psalm 23 activity booklet

(See Student's Book)

Punch holes and tie a ribbon through to keep papers together as in a a booklet. Each child works on their own booklet by tracing over the words of the verses and then following the instructions given on each page.

Activity Sheets:

(See Coloring & Activity Book)

Color page
Be the artist

Prayer/Praise idea:

On the white board, draw little sheep shapes, one for each child. Ask all "God's little sheep" what they may need help and care with today. Are they sick? Are they afraid or worried about something? Do they need help learning something new? As they say their prayer requests, write their name on a sheep. When each one has given their requests, say a general prayer asking God to answer each one's petition. Then draw a happy face on the sheep, showing that God has heard, He loves and cares and will answer His best way.

my notes

(Story 22)

Facing the Big Man

(1 Samuel 17) Lesson topic: COURAGE

A verse to remember:

Be strong and of good courage. Don't be afraid; for the LORD your God will go with you. (Deuteronomy 31:6)

Tell the story idea:

Ask an adult volunteer to act out Goliath and a child to act out David, so that the children can compare sizes as it really happened. If you have a knight or warrior costume, use it for David, as he tries on "King Saul's" armor. Collect little pebbles or stones and a long strip of cloth for the sling, to help children visualise how it might have been used.

Game: David's challenge

Each child is given a piece of old magazine or newspaper. Tell them to crumple it up into a ball as round as possible. Put up a target onto the wall, such as a paper plate, high enough and far enough away to be challenging. Set up an imaginary line and all the children stand behind it, in a row. Then with their best hitting power the children take turns to use their little "Pebble" to aim at and hit the plate. If they miss, they go back to the end of the line to try again. This is a good game to burn out some access energy and also to realize that what little David did was a big challenge and he couldn't have done it without God's power.

Discussion:

- How easy or hard was that for you to do?
- What would have made it easier to hit it the first time around?
- What did you think of when you missed?
- What do you think of when you read the story of David and Goliath?
- When you experience something that is too difficult for you to do alone, what do you do? Who do you go to for help? Who did David go to for help?

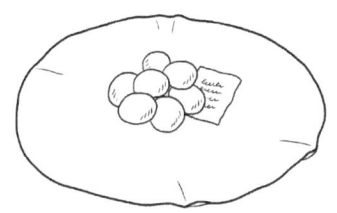
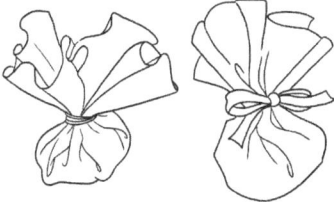

Craft: A bag filled with courage

(See Student's Book)

You will need: brown or beige cloth (or an old sheet) and thin rope or ribbon (about 40 cm per child). Cut out a circle shape of brown cloth for each child as you give them their "little pebbles" illustration and memory verse card, to color and cut out. Remind them how David also picked out five, smooth stones to place in his sling. But today, our stones will be the letters to spell out the word COURAGE. The children can have fun placing their pebbles in order to spell the word. Then show the children how to place their stones and memory verse card into the middle of their cloth. Gather the edges of the circle cloth together to make a little package and secure with an elastic band. Tie the ribbon around the elastic to give a decorative look. Now they're ready for the children to take home as they are reminded to practice courage.

Activity Sheets:

(See Coloring & Activity Book)

Color page
Questions and answers

Prayer/Praise idea:

In advance, collect a rock for each child. Put them in a basket in the middle of the table or floor during your prayer time. Also prepare a big hand shape with the words GOD written on them. As you begin your prayer time, each child picks a rock and writes his name or initials on it (a permanent marker works best). Now they take turns to tell God something that is difficult or hard for them to do on their own, as they place their rock on God's hand and say the words "Dear God, please give me courage!" giving their fear or worry to God to take care of.

my notes

(Story 23)

David's Songs to God

(Psalm 145) Lesson topic: DEVOTION

A verse to remember:

Oh Lord, I will honor and praise Your name, for You are my God and You do such wonderful things. (Isaiah 25:1)

Tell the story idea:

Collect as many musical instruments that you can think of, for the children to act out singing to God. For king David, wear a crown and a long robe. For your throne, add a big pillow and lay a shiny cloth over your chair.

Game: Devotion dance

Use the 4 illustration cards as little stepping boards. You will need one card per child, so you can photocopy them as needed. (You may also want to cover them with clear contact paper first, or put them into a clear plastic sheet, for extra durability.) The cards are: clap hands, jump for joy, lift hands in praise, kneel to pray. To play the game, place them on the floor in the middle of the room. Explain to the children that there are so many different ways you can show your devotion to God, but in this game we'll find out about 5 of them. Start with some dancing. Dancing is a way to glorify and worship God as you use all your muscles and body parts that He has made so amazingly. Put on some music and children dance around the room. When the music stops each child sits on a card and then follows the instructions of what it says to do, as they learn and practice more ways to show devotion to God. Mix up the cards and place them back in the middle to play again and again, for as long as the children enjoy it. You can also play by taking one card out each time the music stops and the child without a card sits and watches or helps to turn off the music next. The last one it is the winner.

Discussion:

- What was your favorite way to show devotion to God? And why?
- Do you do some of these at home, with your parents or family?
- Do you ever do these on your own when no one is looking or there to tell you to do it?

- Who are we doing this for? Ourselves? Others? God?
- How does it benefit us?
  How does it benefit others if they see us doing it?
  How does it make God happy?

Craft: David's harp

(See Student's Book)

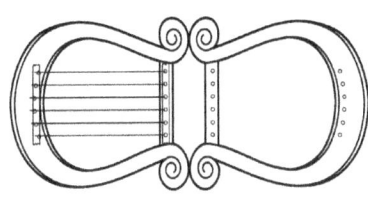

David was a master musician, a poet, a writer of psalms, a worshiper and a man after God's own heart. This cute craft will serve as a great reminder of the life of David, a lowly shepherd boy chosen by God to be the king of Israel. Children color and decorate their harp and then glue it onto thick cardboard for extra strength. Using sticky tape, tape six pieces of yarn onto the illustration, the opposite side of where the children colored. Finally add glue, fold and join both sides of the illustration together forming the harp.

Activity Sheets:

(See Coloring & Activity Book)

Color page
Follow the path

Prayer/Praise idea:

(See Student's Book)

Use the musical instruments cards for this prayer time. Place the cards face down on the table. Each child picks one and prays his request in song (or in talking if they're not comfortable singing) while pretending to play that instrument.

(Story 24)

King Solomon is wise

(1 Kings 3:3-15) Lesson topic: WISDOM

A verse to remember:

If you need more wisdom, ask God for it and He will help you. (James 1:5)

Tell the story idea:

Use two wooden rolling pins from your kitchen and wrap around cloth or paper to use as a pretend scroll. Find some kingly robes and a crown, a long haired wig and a beard, to act out Solomon.

Game 1: Seek God's wisdom

The object of this activity is to show the class why we sometimes make certain choices. But just because something looks good or right doesn't make it always right and good for us. You will need three paper bags or small boxes. Decorate one bag/box beautifully, making it look very attractive. Then add in some small plastic bugs. Make the next bag look ugly but put in a small prizes. Just leave the third bag plain and fill with marshmallows. Have the children take a look at all three bags (just the outside). Take a show of hands to indicate which bag everyone would like to choose from. Then ask 3 volunteers to reach into each bag and take out the item/items inside. Children can now see and realize that when making decisions, we sometimes go with what looks best, but it doesn't mean that it is always the best choice. As we make important decisions, it is a good thing to seek wisdom from God and not rely on our own thoughts. When faced with choices, King Solomon relied on God's wisdom.

Discussion:

- How did you feel when you saw inside the bags?
- Does what we see always mean it's always the best choice or what we think it is?
- How can we know something is right or wrong?
- Who helped Solomon to be so wise?
- Who can help us to make wise choices?

Game 2: No Sight, No Shoes

The object of this game is to demonstrate how difficult it is to find your shoes while blindfolded. In the same manner, we can't live our lives in the right way without God's help and wisdom, to see things as He sees them. Have the children get into a big circle. Ask the children to take off their shoes. Have them place all of their shoes into a big pile. Next, you will need 4 or 5 blindfolds (only allow a small number to play at a time so that no children will get hurt trying to grab their shoes). After the 4 or 5 are blindfolded, tell them that they will have 1 minute to find their shoes and put them on (younger ages can just find their shoes without a blindfold).

Take off their blindfolds so they can see if they got the right ones on properly. After everyone has had a chance to play, gather them all back together as they put on their proper shoes again.

Discussion:

- Was it easy or hard to find your shoes in a big pile when you were blindfolded?
- How is it difficult, trying to do certain things without God's help?
- Explain that there are so many choices in life as you give a few examples like: making friends, choosing a snack, picking clothes to wear, planning an outing for a certain day, when to do your homework, will you make your bed now or later, how do you want your hair done today, choosing a house, finding a job, getting married? Etc.
- If we try to make those choices without God's wisdom it is kind of like trying to find shoes in that big pile with a blindfold on.

Craft: Solomon's scroll.

(See Student's Book for verse card)

For the children to create their own scrolls, you will need two Popsicle sticks and a piece of light brown felt or cloth, 6x8 cm in size, per child. Children take their Popsicle sticks and glue them onto the ends of their felt or cloth with white glue or glue gun. Put them aside to dry for a bit while the children color and decorate their memory verse papers that they can also glue in the middle of the scroll. Now let the children roll up their scrolls, and then unroll them again to review their verse.

Activity Sheets:

(See Coloring & Activity Book)

Color page
What is wisdom?

Prayer/Praise idea: Kingly prayers

Use a dress-up crown or make one of your own if you don't have one, to use for this prayer time. While each child prays, they get to wear the King's crown. In turn, each one prays something like: "Dear God. Give me wisdom in ...... (child chooses what he wants God's wisdom for, whether learning something new, for his school or homework, learning to ride a bike, learning to read, etc.) and passes the crown to the person sitting next to them who continues with the same.

(Story 25)

A Temple for God

(1 Kings 4-7) Lesson topic: WORSHIP

A verse to remember:

How great is the Lord, and how much we should praise him. (Psalms 48:1)

Tell the story idea:

Use some sheets, ropes and pegs to make an indoor tent (or better yet, use a play tent if you have one). Children act out and pretend that they're going into the temple (tent) to pray and worship God. Use a crown when you talk about King Solomon.

Game: Build a temple

Bring a big box of Lego, Duplo or wooden blocks. Have the kids spend a bit of time creating and building a temple as if they were Solomon's workers, as you put on some worship songs for the kids to sing along with. Pick a child to pretend to be King Solomon (wearing a crown and red robe), drawing up the plans and giving orders on how to build it.

Discussion:

- Did you enjoy building God's temple?
- If you were really building God's house, what would you make sure to do or not do?
- Where did Solomon get his instructions from, on how to build the temple?
- What things can we get God's help and instructions with?
- Why did Solomon build a temple?
- Who enjoyed the music playing while building?
- What kind of music was it? Did it have something to do with the temple?
- At home, do you play or do things while you're thinking about God or while singing or praising?

Craft: Temple puzzle

(See Student's Book)

Color and decorate the temple puzzle pieces, with yellow, gold and glitter. Then cut them out on the gray lines and glue them in place onto the blank temple page.

Activity Sheets:

(See Coloring & Activity Book)

Color page
Praises to God

Prayer/Praise idea: A temple time

Prepare a quick made up tent with sheets or cardboard boxes, and call it your "temple". Tell the children to pretend that they are going inside to kneel and pray to their king Jesus, as if they would to a real king. Place a picture frame of Jesus on a chair inside the tent. Each child takes a turn to go inside, kneel before the King, bow down and tell Jesus what they are thankful for and how much they love and adore Him.

my notes

(Story 26)

God feeds Elijah

(1 Kings 16,17) Lesson topic: ENDURANCE

A verse to remember:

If you have endurance, you will finish what you've started and receive God's blessings. (Hebrews 10:36)

Tell the story idea:

Collect some umbrellas, small cloths or cardboard boxes for the children to act out Elijah hiding from the wicked queen. Children can also find any other appropriate hiding spots such as under tables or chairs, behind a cupboard, etc. Bring along some black outfits for the teachers to wear as ravens bringing a little snack of bread and hot dogs cut into little pieces. Use a blue sheet as the brook and pretend to dip your hands or face in to drink.

Game: Ice-cream endurance

Get a sturdy large zip-lock bag and fill it halfway with ice. Add six tablespoons of rock salt. In a separate smaller-size plastic bag, pour in one cup of milk, two tablespoons of sugar, half a teaspoon of vanilla, and a handful of chocolate chips. Seal the smaller bag with a knot or rubber band and put it inside the larger bag (seal that one too). Shake the bag for 10 minutes, passing it around with each child taking a turn. It will seem like forever to the children, but when the time's up, they'll find their perseverance has paid off – with homemade chocolate-chip ice cream!

Discussion:

- How long do you think it took to make the ice cream? (Each child gives an estimate and then tell them the exact time it took)
- Did you feel like giving up? Why or why not?
- Do you sometimes do things that take a long time? Like what?
- Why do you do them?
- What good came out of our endurance today?
- What other good things can come out when we work hard and are patient to wait?

Craft: Peg Bird

(See Student's Book)

You will need a clothes peg and a pair of googly eyes for each child. Children paint their peg black and then let it sit to dry.

Give each child their bird illustration and instruct them to color or paint the bird's wings and tail black and the beak and feet bright yellow. Cut them out, then glue each piece onto to the dry peg as shown here. The children also color and cut out the piece of bread and meat and hang them inside the peg, along with their verse card as a reminder that God blesses those who endure.

Activity Sheets:

(See Coloring & Activity Book)

Color page
God provided

Prayer/Praise idea: Blow a bubble prayer

Take a little bubble blowing set and pass it around the circle, giving each child a turn. Each child blows a bubble and says something like "Jesus, be with ….(say a name of a family member or sick person, someone who is in need)", then watch the bubble as it rises and vanishes, just like our prayers get sent up to God. God takes them and answers them in His good time.

(Story 27)

A widow in need

(1 Kings 17:7-16) Lesson topic: UNSELFISHNESS

A verse to remember:

Don't just look out for yourself and think about your own good, but also think about the good of others. (Philippians 2:4)

Tell the story idea:

Wear an apron and come with a pack of flour and a mixing bowl, a little oil and make some bread dough as you tell the story.

Game 1: Pass it on

All children line up facing sideways. Give a ball to the first player and have him roll it gently through his legs to the person behind him. As soon as he's done, he rushes to the back of the line waiting again his turn with the ball. This game shows that when you give, you receive and you always get back in return. You passed the ball on, but always got it back again.

Discussion:

- Now pretend that the ball you were giving was your favorite toy or your favorite snack that you shared with someone who didn't get any. How easy would it have been to give it away?
- Did you know that you were going to get it back later when you went to the back of the line? Did that make it easier to go?
- It is easier to give away things that you like or that you don't like so much?
- Which do you think bring the most rewards or blessings?
- Why does God encourage us to give and share with others? Is it always for their sakes?

Game 2: Jars of oil

Collect as many plastic bottles or cartons that you can, from milk, juice, mayonnaise, etc. Put them together in a big box with all the lids off. Now empty them out and kids can have fun matching the bottles with their lids, pretending it was all the jars of oil that were multiplied.

Craft: Verse puzzle

(See Student's Book)

Give each child their "loaf of bread" to color and cut out. Begin with the outer shape and then cut into slices. Now the slices will be all mixed up, so the children can glue their bread puzzle back together again. Once done, recite the verse together.

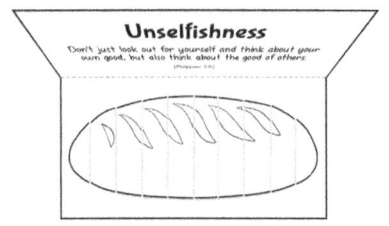

Activity Sheets:

(See Coloring & Activity Book)

Color page
What happened?

Prayer/Praise idea: Painting Prayer

Use some non-toxic finger paints for this prayer time. Hang a big sheet of paper in front of the class or on the white board and the children take turns to dab their finger into one color of their choice, make a little pattern on the paper as they pray or thank God for something of that color. For example, one child picks the color red, dips his finger into the paint, then makes a red circle on the paper and thanks God for red apples because it's his favorite fruit, etc. Keep going till all the children have had a turn and you have a painting masterpiece of prayers to God.

my notes

(Story 28)

Naaman gets help

(2 Kings 5:1-15) Lesson topic: DETERMINATION

A verse to remember:

Keep your eyes focused on what is right to do. Look straight ahead to what is good. (Proverbs 4:25)

Tell the story idea:

Prepare a bucket with a plastic dolly and draw spots all over it with a whiteboard marker that washes off easily later. As Naaman is washing and as you're telling the story, dip the dolly into a bucket or bowl of water. The children can take turns to dip it in and out. Keep doing this till the seventh time, then scrub off the dots so it's as good as new and Naaman is "healed".

Game: Seven is heaven

All children sit down in a circle. Tap a child on the head to start. He calls out the number 1, next player 2, 3, 4, etc. all the way to number 7. The child that calls out the number 7 jumps up with his hands in the air and says "Hurray! I'm healed!" The next child continues the game again starting from number 1 and continuing with each seventh child shouting "Hurray!"

Discussion:

- What if you had to do something or ask something 7 times before you got an answer?
- What if you had to try climbing a mountain 6 times till the last time you finally made it?
- Or you got mistakes on your spelling words 6 times till finally the 7th time you got them right?
- What is it like waiting 7 days till your birthday?
- All those things are difficult and they teach us what?
- What does determination make you think of? Or what does it sound like?
- Can you think of some things that you need determination for each day? Give some examples.

Craft: Naaman's determination

(See Student's Book)

Give each child the illustration page to color and cut onto the gray lines. For the Naaman illustration, fold on the dotted lines, place a Popsicle stick in the middle and glue together. Cut a slit in the background page, on the dotted lines, to place Naaman inside.

The children can dip him in and out of the water (pretend water drawn on the page) while holding the Popsicle stick from the back of the picture. Practice doing it seven times and then taking Naaman all the way out and turning him over, to make him well and happy.

Activity Sheets:

(See Coloring & Activity Book)

Color page
Find the shapes

Prayer/Praise idea:

Prepare in advance some large numbers 1-7. Give each child one of the numbers that he places on the table right in front of him/her. Number 1 child chooses an action and prays for a request that he wants to pray for or that the teacher gives him. Example: "Dear God, please give me determination!" He repeats the prayer as he does his action, for example claps his hands, then children 2-6 repeat and do the same thing. Finally child 7 jumps up and says "Thank You God for determination!" or whatever thanks he can give to go along with the prayer request. Then for child 8, start again at number one and keep going till all the children have had a turn to pray and do their action.

my notes

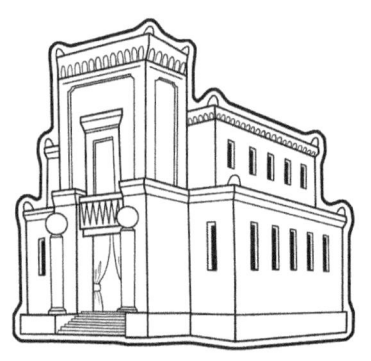

(Story 29)

Little king Joash

(2 Kings 11,12) Lesson topic: TEAMWORK

A verse to remember:

Two people are better than one. They can help each other in everything they do. (Ecclesiastes 4:9a)

Tell the story idea:

A treasure chest toy or a fancy box could be used for telling the story of Joash. Have children drop coins into the box as you tell the story of the people bringing money to the temple. Make sure you have lots of small change so the children can hear the fun clinking.

Game: Treasure hunt

(See Student's Book)

Use the two pages of picture and preposition cards as clues of where to hide (for the teachers) and find (for the kids) the next hidden pictures that will lead to the treasure (or you can make some of your own if you prefer). End with a treasure of a few play coins per child, spray-painted gold beforehand.

Discussion:

- Was it easy to find the treasure?
- What made it easy?
- Is it easy to follow instructions when your mom and dad tell you to do something?
- Is it difficult when there are other things you want to do instead?
- Do you think your parents will ask you to do wrong things?
- What do you think could help to make it easier for you to obey and follow?

Game 2: Temple repairs

(See Student's Book)

For this game you will need coins, the temple puzzle illustration and a little treasure chest or decorative little box that you may have. Prepare the puzzle beforehand by coloring and cutting it out into as many little pieces as you want, depending on how many children you have or the level that you want. Use the questions below or include some of your own for the children to answer. If they answer it correctly, they get to put a coin inside the box to help pay for temple repairs and can add a puzzle piece to rebuild it.

Questions:
1. What book of the Bible is this story found?
2. How old was Joash when he became King?
3. What was the most important thing King Joash did?
4. Where did little Joash grow up?
5. Who took care of him?
6. Who trained Joash and taught him about God?
7. How did Joash learn so many things?
8. Why did Joash have to hide from his grandmother?
9. Who was Priest Jehoida?
10. Who worshiped idols?
11. Who did Joash worship and serve?
12. How did he help the people worship the true God?
13. What did Joash do with a treasure chest?
14. What did the people put in the chest?
15. What was the money in the chest used for?

Craft: Chest envelope

(See Student's Book)

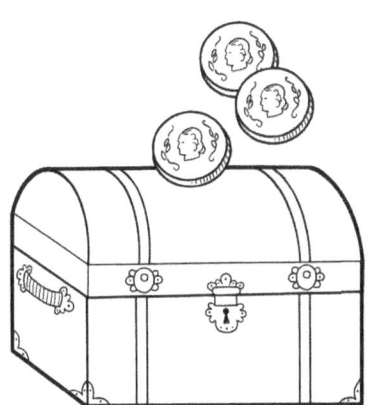

Children make a little treasure chest just like King Joash had for the temple. Have them color and decorate their chest, cut it out and add glue on the two sides to keep it closed. Cut a little slit for the locket and fold over the lid. For the coins, color and cut each one out, then write the verse: "Those who follow my ways are happy." (Proverbs 8:23) one word on each coin. They can practice putting the verse in the right order, then put their little "treasures" safe into their chests and have them ready to take home.

Activity Sheets:

(See Coloring & Activity Book)

Color page
Dot to dot

Prayer/Praise idea:

Use any game board that you have. Place post-its on each square with little prayer requests written or drawn on them. When children roll the die and land on a square, they get to pray for that request. You can keep going till all the children have had a turn or till one child gets to the end of the game board. At the end of the game, raise your hands and praise the Lord together for answering your prayers.

my notes

(Story 30)

Three Brave men

(Daniel 3) Lesson topic: CONVICTION

A verse to remember:

We have gained confidence and boldly speak God's message without fear. (Philippians 1:14)

Tell the story idea:

Bring a candle to show how hot the fire furnace was. If you have a heater or fireplace, sit right next to it, to feel the heat. Take a cardboard box for your pretend furnace and fill it with crumpled up red crepe paper as the fire. Use 4 little Playmobile characters (or other toy people you may have available) to put into and out of your "furnace" as you tell the story.

Game: Conviction jumps

All children sit in a circle. Leader calls out different things like: "Likes to sing, has a brother, has a sister, combs their own hair, likes to dance, has a pet, reads their Bible, etc." All the children who can relate to one of those or does one of those things, jumps up real high and says "I do!"

Discussion:

- Did everyone jump up for exactly the same reasons?
- Does everyone like the same things or do the same things as everyone else?
- Did you feel brave or shy as you jumped up to tell us about yourself?
- God made us each special and different, and we can be bold to show who we are and what we do. Will someone make fun of you because you have a pet or a brother or sister?
- Will people think you're strange because you like eating cereal for breakfast?
- Should we worry about what people think of us?
- Can we be bold and strong to show who we are, and what we believe in?
- Let's be confident in God too. Don't you think He's pleased when you pray, read your Bible and tell others about Him?

Craft: Fiery furnace

(See Student's Book)

Give each child the illustration to color and cut out. Glue some red and yellow color paper leaf shapes onto the fire flap and then add some glue to the back, on the bottom part, so that you can open and close it. Read out the verse together as you remember about conviction.

59

Activity Sheets:

(See Coloring & Activity Book)

Color page
Hidden message

Prayer/Praise idea:

Prepare little lit candles, the type that sits on the table easily without tipping over. In turn, each child brings a candle close (keeping safety in mind) as they say their prayers or thanks to God. At the end when everyone has had a chance to pray, place the candles in the middle of the table and turn off all the lights as you raise your hands and thank God for His protection.

(Story 31)

Daniel prays to God

(Daniel 6) Lesson topic: PEER-PRESSURE

A verse to remember:

Be sure to do what is right and good in the sight of the Lord. (Deuteronomy 6:18a)

Tell the story idea:

Bring with you as many little or big play lions (stuffed animals or plastic toys, puppets, etc.) to act out the story with. Then use a Playmobile or Lego man for Daniel. Use a see through bowl or box to throw Daniel in. Fill it with a few rocks or gray paper or cloth, along with the lions all around him.

Game 1: Action Poem

Children can have fun learning this little rhyme together, using their hands. Keep doing it until all the children have learned it well and can take it home to share with their families.

This is my mother, who helps me at play. (raise thumb)
This is my father, who works all the day. (raise second finger)
This is my brother, so strong and so tall. (raise third finger)
This is my sister, who likes to play ball. (raise fourth finger)
And this is me; I'm happy to say (raise fifth finger)
Together our family kneels down to pray. (close fist)

Discussion:

- Do you pray every day?
- Daniel prayed 3 times a day. How many times do you think you pray each day?
- Do you see your brothers and sisters and parents pray?
- Do you always pray together or sometimes do you also pray alone?
- What time of the day do you pray most often? Why is that?
- When do you forget to pray?

Game 2: Prayerful chairs

This game is played similarly to the popular "musical chairs" game. Place the chairs in a circle, one less than the number of children. Have the kids march around the chairs as you sing a chant of the story of Daniel:

Daniel prayed and didn't delay.
He prayed faithfully, 3 times a day.
Then Daniel went along his way
But not without remembering to pray.

When you end the chant, the children all run to a chair and sit down. The one who doesn't make it in time to a chair tells the other children of one thing that he thinks Daniel prayed for, or talks about his favorite way to pray, and then sits out to help sing the chant for the next round. At each round, remove a chair and continue to play until there is only one person left who can act out Daniel praying.

Craft 1: Lion mask

(See Student's Book)

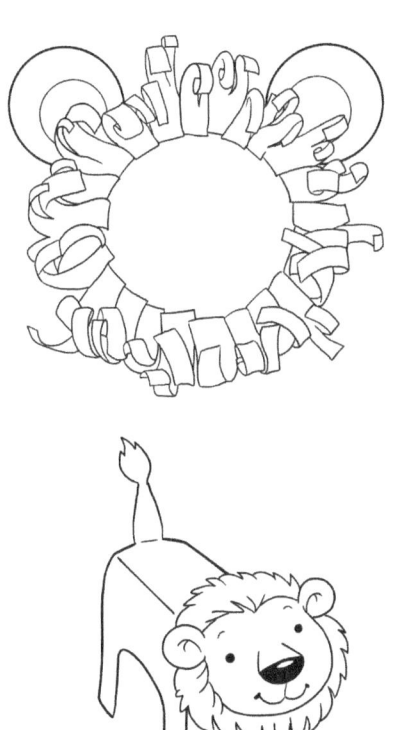

You will need a paper plate, with the middle part cut out, for each child. Have them color the lion's ears illustration and glue on the top of their plate. Then cut out a whole bunch of brown and yellow paper strips for the children to glue around the edges of their plate. It makes things easier if they put glue onto the plate instead of on each strip. And If you have extra time, help them to curl up their strips with scissors, to make it look like a real lion's mane. Now all the lions can quote the verse together, using their little verse card.

Craft 2: A stand-up lion

(See Student's Book)

Use the illustrations provided, for each child to color and cut out on the gray lines. Fold on the dotted lines, the head and tail facing up and the legs facing down, as shown in example. Now the children have their own stand-up lions as they retell the story.

Activity Sheets:

(See Coloring & Activity Book)

Color page
Continue drawing

Prayer/Praise idea:

Daniel prayed 3 times a day, so draw 3 clocks on your white board or on paper plates, letting the children know that you will pray 3 times during your lesson time. Draw the times that you will stop to pray, as well as what you will pray for during those prayer breaks, so that the children can remind you of the time when they see the clock.

my notes

(Story 32)

Nehemiah Rebuilds

(Nehemiah 1,2) Lesson topic: PERSEVERANCE

A verse to remember:

Let us not be weary in doing things that are good. (Galatians 6:9a)

Tell the story idea:

Bring some tools that you may need for rebuilding the walls as well as a small ladder to show that they needed to reach up high, a real brick if you can find one, cement made out of flour and water to show how they used it to stick the bricks together so it could be a strong wall, etc.

Game: Build up your perseverance

Hide small cut out rectangular papers (red or brown) pretending that they're bricks, all over the room. Send the kids to find them and bring them back to the table. Divide up the bricks evenly to each child. Build a tower together, gluing their bricks onto a cardboard box that you will pretend is your wall. As each puts up their brick, they express something that they're learning to do at home that takes perseverance.

Discussion:

- How did it feel when we all worked together to build the walls?
- What if you had to do it on your own, would it be more difficult? Why is that?
- What are some things that may distract you from doing a job you have to do?
- What do you do to keep from getting distracted?
- What is something that helps you to get to your job right away and persevering till it's done?

Craft: Build up the walls

(See Student's Book)

Have children color or paint all the illustration pages. Then cut out the pieces that go in front, fold on the dotted lines, then glue them onto the background page as shown in example. Read the verse together.

Activity Sheets:

(See Coloring & Activity Book)

Color page
Finish the job

Prayer/Praise idea:

(See Student's Book)

Use the illustration pictures of prayer requests for this prayer time together. After the pictures are colored and cut out, place them in the middle of the table face down. Each child takes a turn to pick a card and pray for the request or something on that topic.

my notes

(Story 33)

Esther saves her people

(book of Esther) Lesson topic: BEAUTY

A verse to remember:

"True beauty comes from inside you. It is the beauty of a gentle and quiet spirit." (1 Peter 3:3-4)

Tell the story idea:

It's probably not too difficult to find a princess dress, a princess crown and scepter. If they don't fit you, then any little girl would probably love to volunteer to get up in front of everyone and wear the costume as you tell the story about Queen Esther.

Game: Before the king

All children sit in a circle. The leader calls out for a volunteer who gets blindfolded. During that time one other child is chosen to be "it" and to go before the king. The leader points to the child chosen who will go out of the room quietly. The rest of the children disperse and change places. Now the first child who had a blindfold on, takes it off and tries to guess who went bravely before the king (out of the room). If he guesses correctly, he gets to choose the next "Esther" to leave the room. The next person blindfolded is the child who left the room.

Discussion:

- What part of the game did you like the best? Being the one blindfolded, going out of the room or guessing?
- Who in your life is beautiful?
- What makes them beautiful?
- Who is someone that you know that is beautiful on the inside?
- What do you think makes them that way?
- List all the things that you think makes a girl beautiful on the outside.
- Now list some things that can make you beautiful on the inside.
- Can boys also be beautiful or handsome on the inside? How?
- Can they be beautiful on the outside? Why not? (God made men to be handsome, each in their own way.)

Craft 1: Queen Esther paper doll

(See Student's Book)

Use the illustration page provided for each child to color and cut out. Then children will have a blast retelling the story of Esther with their mini paper doll.

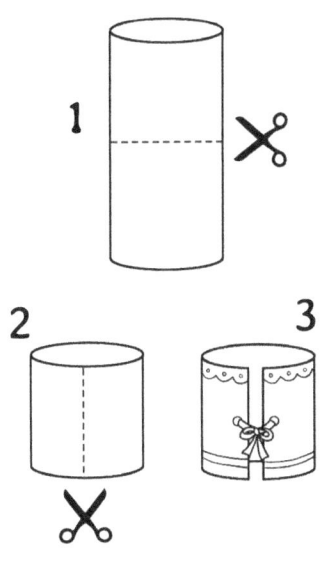

Craft 2: Queenly (or Kingly) wrist bands

You will need half an empty toilet paper roll for each child, some thin ribbon and decorative lace, fancy buttons, beads or anything you can use for decorating. Cut the rolls in half, giving one half to each child (1). Then cut again, this time through the side, so that it opens up and you can place it flat in front of you (2). Children paint their rolls, then glue a piece of lace onto it to make it look more royal. They can also choose a fancy bead or button to glue in the middle. Glue the verse onto the inside of the bracelet so they can be reminded of God's beauty when they take it off or put in on again. Punch a hole into each end of the roll and use a little piece of ribbon to string it through and tie it onto their wrist (3).

Activity Sheets:

(See Coloring & Activity Book)

Color page
Puzzle pieces

Prayer/Praise idea: Mystery bag prayer

Fill up a bag with plenty of little toy objects (see list below, but feel free to add or change accordingly). Each time a child digs into the bag, he pulls out the first object he feels and prays for something related to it. When he is finished praying, you can either place the object back into the bag (if you have many kids in your class), or put it aside for next time. Here are some ideas of objects to include, as well as related prayer requests:

1. House/furniture: Pray or thank God for something at home
2. Pencil: Ask God to bless your teacher or help you do good school
3. Dolly: Pray or thank God for something specific about your family
4. Heart: Pray or thank God for your friends
5. Happy face: Thank God for something that makes you feel happy.
6. Sad face: Tell God you are sorry for something that you did wrong
7. Food: Thank God for your favorite food. Pray for people who don't have enough to eat
8. Band-aid: Ask God to heal someone who is sick or hurt.

(Story 34)

Jonah and the Fish

(Jonah 1-3) Lesson topic: AVAILABILITY

A verse to remember:

"I desire to do Your will, dear God, because Your Words are in my heart." (Psalm 40:8)

Tell the story idea:

You will need a blue balloon and a little Playmobile or Lego men for Jonah. Prepare a few paper fins and a tail to glue during your lesson, (for after you blow up the balloon). Have a marker on hand to draw the whale's eyes and mouth, as well as a little toy boat, a small bucket or baby bathtub of water as you're telling the story.

Game 1: Hide and seek

All the children hide (as best as they can) while the teacher and a helper count. The teacher will pretend to be God calling Jonah and the helper will be the whale under a big blue sheet (if you have one). Once they finish counting, God goes to the middle of the room trying to spot anyone that moves from their hiding place. As soon as he notices someone, he calls them out by their name and says, "Suzy, go to Nineveh!" That child comes running back to base trying not to get caught by the whale who crawls around the room. Anyone caught sits down at the table. The teacher and helper continue to replay until all the children are caught.

Discussion:

- Who had fun? What was your favorite part about the game? What was your least favorite part?
- How would you feel if every time you hid somewhere the person looking for you knew exactly where you were?
- Who can we never hide from? And why?
- Have you ever started playing hide and seek when your parents asked you to do something?
- How would that work out for you or for them?
- Our story today is about a man who tried to play hide from God, only he wasn't having any fun...

Game 2: Pin Jonah onto the whale

Take the little Jonah picture; color and plastify it for extra durability. Now draw a huge whale on a piece of paper and tape it to the wall so that your children can reach it easily. Blindfold the children, one at a time, and have them take turns trying to tape Jonah onto the whale.

Craft: A whale wheel

(See Student's Book)

Give the illustration page to each child for them to color and cut out on the gray lines. Combine them with a brad brass. Then the children can have fun retelling the story of Jonah as they turn the wheel:
1. Jonah running away from God
2. Jonah thrown into the sea
3. Jonah praying and saying sorry
4. Now Jonah running to obey God

Activity Sheets:

(See Coloring & Activity Book)

Color page
Raise the sails

Prayer/Praise idea:

Prepare a big baking tray filled with sand or rice, salt or flour, etc. Pour the salt into the tray until the bottom is completely covered. Smooth over to make the surface flat. Now use a lollypop stick or an end of a wooden spoon to write an initial or to draw somebody or something you would like to ask God to bless. Each child has a turn to draw in the "sand" and pray his prayer. As the child ends his prayer and says "Amen," he smooths out the salt for the next child to pray.

(Story 35)

The King is Born

(Luke 2:1-2) Lesson topic: GOD'S LOVE

A verse to remember:
"God loved us so much, that He sent us His only Son." John 3:16a

Tell the story idea:
Collect a baby doll and a pillowcase to wrap the baby into as you talk about baby Jesus. You will need a cardboard box and a toy donkey, cow, sheep and chicken. The box can be used twofold: for the dolly's manger bed and for the barn, to fit in all the animals, depending on what part of the story you're telling at the time.

Game: Ball bounce Praise
Children stand in the shape of a square and hold on to the ends of a sheet, including the four corners. Put a light ball into the center of the sheet and all the children lift it up in unison as they bounce the ball up. Every time it goes up high, the children can send up a praise to God for His love. If the ball falls to the floor, the leader calls out a problem, picks it up and places it back onto the sheet while the children shout out another praise related to the problem or difficulty.

Discussion:
- How did it feel to praise God?
- How do you think He feels when we praise and thank Him?
- Is it difficult to thank God when we are thinking about problems and difficulties?
- Why should we still choose to praise Him during those times?
- Did someone thank YOU today? How did it make you feel?
- What can we be the happiest for today, in relation to our story?

Craft: In a manger
(See Student's Book)

Use the illustrations provided for the children to color and cut out onto the gray lines. Fold the paper on the bottom dotted lines facing up. Color the front flaps that are facing the front and then tape them on the sides to keep them in place. Take the animals, Joseph, Mary and baby Jesus illustrations and place them into the folded flaps as you wish. Fold the whole illustration in the center and stand it up on the table, for children to tell their own "Baby Jesus" story, while taking the figures in and out of the flaps.

Activity Sheets:

(See Coloring & Activity Book)

Color page
Make the same

Prayer/Praise idea: Gift box pass

Since we're on the topic of the birth of Jesus, we can celebrate His birthday. What do we give to the birthday person? (gifts) So what kind of gifts do we want to give to Jesus? Take a big cardboard box that has been decorated in advance (with wrapping paper, a big bow or ribbon tied on top). With a permanent marker, write down a whole bunch of one-sentence praises to God. During your prayer time, play some soft happy music and each child takes a turn with the box, to read one of the praises to God, then pass it on to the next player, who also takes the box and finds a phrase to thank God for. Children keep passing it on till all the kids have had a turn to thank God for something written on the box. It's okay if some are repeated, God loves to hear them all and many times over.

(Story 36)

The Wise men visit

(Matthew 2:1-12) Lesson topic: ADMIRATION

A verse to remember:

"I will honor You, my God and King. I will praise Your name forever and ever." (Psalm 145:1)

Tell the story idea:

Use little chocolates and candies wrapped in fancy shiny papers as the gifts. Collect some fancy, shiny robes or scarves to dress up the "wisemen". Make some stars for some of the children to hold up high.

Game 1: Follow the star

Play this game as you talk about the wisemen following the star. Close the curtains or shutters and invite a volunteer to point flashlights to the wall or floor. The rest of the children take turns stepping on or touching the reflected light on the floor or walls. The idea is to keep the children moving, all the while understanding the concept of keeping a close eye to following the star. The children waiting for their turn can be the cheerleaders.

Discussion:

- How was it following the star?
- It was fun for a little while but imagine following the star for days and even months.
- Why did the wise men bring gifts to Jesus?
- What are some things to do to show our love for someone?
- Why did they bring such expensive gifts to Jesus?
- What are some gifts that you've given away to someone special?
- How do you feel when someone gives you a gift or says something nice to you?

Game 2: Wiseman, wiseman, Camel

Pick one child to be it first. The other children sit in a circle on the ground facing inward. The child who is "it" walks around the circle tapping heads and saying "Wiseman" on as many heads as he wants. As soon as he taps a head and says "Camel" instead, he starts to run around the circle. "Camel" jumps up and chases "it" trying to tag him. If "it" sits down in Camel's spot before being tagged, then Camel is the new "it". But if Camel tags him, then he has another turn being "it".

my notes

Craft 1: Star candle holder

(See Student's Book)

Use the star illustrations for the kids to cut out, color or paint. Add some shiny glitter onto their edges. Glue the small star over the big star with a dab of glue in the middle. Then use a glass jar (from yogurts or puddings) for each child to decorate. A few decoration ideas: Add a row of glitter around the jar, tie a ribbon or bow around it, add a star shaped button in the front of the bow, place star stickers all around, etc. Add a dab of glue (a glue gun works best) in the middle of the star and gently place the jar on top and leave to dry a few minutes. Put in the finishing touch by adding a candle to each jar.

Craft 2: The Wisemen's gifts

(See Student's Book)

Use the illustration of the 3 wisemen. Children color and cut them out, then glue each one onto a small colorful rectangle paper. Glue these three rectangle papers onto a bigger colorful or patterned folded card paper. Cut out and glue the verse inside the card as you all read it out loud together. Glue a wrapped up candy or chocolate onto each of the wisemen's hands. The next time the children thank and worship God for something, they can enjoy one of the chocolates or candies.

Activity Sheets:

(See Coloring & Activity Book)

Color page
Find the gifts

Prayer/Praise idea: Jumping stars

(See Student's Book)

Make a star shape out of colored paper for each child. Have them write or draw on it, one thing that they love most about the Christmas story. Now place them all in the middle of the floor and the children can dance around them to a fun Christmas song. As soon as the music stops, the children jump onto the star closest to them. Whatever star they land on, they praise and thank God for it. Keep going for as long as the children enjoy it.

my notes

(Story 37)

At the temple

(Luke 2:41-52) Lesson topic: GOD'S WORD

A verse to remember:

"The teaching of God's Word gives understanding." (Psalm 119:130)

Tell the story idea:

Bring the biggest books you can find and the most Bibles you have, to compare the biggest and fanciest books, explaining that it's what's inside the books that counts. Share a few interesting facts about the Bible (for example: How many books are in the Bible? Which books talk about the life of Jesus, etc.) If you have a bit of time beforehand put together a scroll, made from kitchen paper towel rolls or rolling pins, along with sheets of paper rolled on to it, to show how books looked like in Jesus' day.

Game 1: Pin Jesus in the temple

(See Student's Book)

Get a large sheet of paper and draw walls and pillars for inside the temple, see example picture. Each child colors and cuts out his little Jesus figure and takes a turn to be blindfolded. They have to try and place Jesus in the middle of the temple on the footprints. The winner is the child who pins Jesus closest to the footprints. At the end, each child gets to take their little Jesus figure home.

Game 2: Bible charades

Use a children's Bible book and crack the book open to read one phrase or sentence from that page, without anyone seeing what story it is. Let the children guess the story. If a child guesses right, it's his turn to crack the book open and read something from another page for the others to guess. For younger children, instead of reading from the children's Bible, they can give hint words, or describe something in the picture; for example if the story is about Baby Moses, a hint word good be "basket" or "river Nile", etc.

Discussion:

- How did you get so smart?
- How did it make you feel to know so many Bible stories?
- Do you memorize Bible verses? Do you know why you do it?
- Do you take time to read and learn from the Bible each day?
- What else do we do besides reading the Bible?

- What is even more important?
- How can we show that we love Jesus and His Word?

Craft: Jesus in the temple lantern

(See Student's Book)

Color and cut out the illustration on the gray lines. Fold over all the dotted lines and then glue in place, as a cube. Punch a hole on the top dots and tie a little string or ribbon if you want to hang it up. Or you could stand it up instead. This little lantern will remind you that you can be smart in God's Word even as a young child, like Jesus was when he amazed all the temple priests.

Activity Sheets:

(See Coloring & Activity Book)

Color page
Match the shadows

Prayer/Praise idea:

Beforehand, prepare little papers with simple prayers written on them, related to learning from God's Word. Then place them in-between the pages of a big picture Bible. During your prayer time, pass the Bible around, and the children in turn, "dig in", open the book, find a paper and read it out. If your children don't read yet, you could draw little pictures instead of things for them to pray for. Then they look at the picture page (where the request was placed) and thank God for something on that page, whether it's an object or an animal or a character they would like to thank God for.

my notes

(Story 38)

Talk About Jesus

(John 1:19-34) Lesson topic: BOLDNESS

A verse to remember:
"May you speak the Word of God with all boldness." (Acts 4:29)

Tell the story idea:
Serve a small snack of honey on crackers. Explain that John the Baptist ate locusts (show a picture of locusts and talk about what they are) and wild honey with other things than crackers of course. Bring a kitchen tray along with a cup of water to pour into the tray. Use small plastic toy people to act out and show how baptism works. If you have a picture of a dove or a toy dove, bring that too.

Game: Ball to ball
Everyone stands or sits in a circle. A small ball gets passed around from person to person. Explain that you're pretending that this is John the Baptist. Do a whole turn and then bring in a bigger ball, pretending that it's Jesus. Continue passing around the small ball but now also including the bigger ball. Explain that John is like the smaller ball preparing the way for Jesus. Jesus is the big ball and follows the smaller ball. If the bigger ball catches up with the smaller one, then it's time for them to meet. Retell the story in your own words of how John and Jesus met.

Discussion:
- What was John the Baptist's job?
- Was it an important job? Why or why not?
- What did John need in order to speak loudly to all the people about Jesus?
- What happened after John and Jesus met that day?
- If you're not baptizing people like John did, what do you need boldness for today?
- How can we receive boldness and from where?

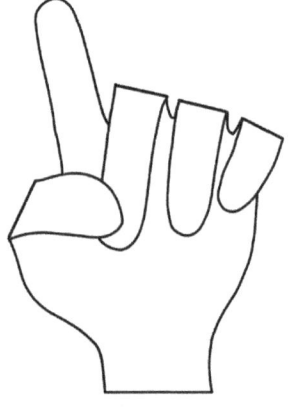

Craft 1: Preaching hand
(See Student's Book)
Use the big hand print provided (or children can make their own if they prefer). Color, then cut it out. Fold all the fingers down (frontward) except for the pointer finger, which shows John preaching about God's Word. Glue the verse card onto the palm of the hand and read it out together as you "preach it" loudly and boldly.

Craft 2: John baptizes Jesus

(See Student's Book)

Color and cut out the illustrations of John the Baptist, Jesus and the frogs. Fold flap frontward on the dotted lines. Glue on the sides and then cut out the little oval shape to make a hole. Glue the frogs onto the front of the flap, as shown in the example. Glue Jesus figure onto a Popsicle stick and place inside the flap with the stick coming out of the hole. Now the children can lift Jesus in and out of the water as He's getting baptized.

Activity Sheets:

(See Coloring & Activity Book)

Color page
Puzzle pieces

Prayer/Praise idea:

Prepare a bowl of clean water and a towel. Pass the bowl around the table and each child dips his hands in and washes his face, then says "Thank You God, for washing away my sins!" Pass the towel around for the children to dry up.

(Story 39)

Jesus picks His disciples

(Mark 3:13-19) Lesson topic: FOLLOWING JESUS

A verse to remember:

"Jesus left us an example to follow and to do as He did." (1 Peter 2:21b)

Tell the story idea:

Use 12 empty plastic bottles or just 12 bottle tops with happy faces drawn on each one, to use as you talk about Jesus' disciples. Use a bigger bottle for Jesus or a jar if you're using bottle tops. Of course if you have more time you can dress them up by gluing cloth or paper on top.
Before the lesson, prepare name tags for as many children as you will be expecting. On each name tag write one of the 12 disciples' names. There can be doubles depending on how many children attend. The children wear their name tags with their "new disciple name" during the whole lesson, and can call each other that name, as a way to familiarize themselves with the disciples' names.

Mnemonic:

An easy way to remember the disciples' names is to create a mnemonic. For example Stamp the Toast with Peanut Butter and 4 Jams stands for Simon, Thaddaeus, Andrew, Matthew, Philip (STAMP) Thomas (T for toast), Peter (P for peanut), Bartholomew, (B for butter), John, James, Judas and James (4 jams).

Game 1: Stepping stones

In this activity the children take steps that represent things they can do to come closer to Jesus. Use some sheets of papers as little "stepping stones". Lay them on the floor, making a path that leads to a picture of Jesus. Children follow an action that you call out, and then step onto the first stone. Each time they follow the actions (of something Jesus says to do) they get to move forward one step (one stone).

Some ideas of following Jesus actions (for the teacher to call out): pray, lift your hands and praise, clap your hands for God's greatness, jump up and down and cheer, think of something positive, give a hug, give a smile, tell someone "Jesus loves you!", take time to listen (cup your hands to your ears), forgive someone who's done wrong to you, read God's Word, study God's Word, love your neighbor, give to others in need.

Discussion:

- How did it feel to make your way close to Jesus?
- Can we get close to Jesus by just doing one of those things?
- How do you follow Jesus at home, or with your family?
- How did the disciples follow Jesus?
- Why did they have to leave their jobs or families?
- Do we have to do that in order to follow Jesus? Or can we follow Him while doing the things we need to do?
- Why do we want to get closer to Jesus?
- Does following Jesus and doing those things make us happy? Why or why not?

Craft 1: 12 disciples accordion book

(See Student's Book)

Use the illustration page for each child. Cut on the gray lines and fold accordion style on the dotted lines. One side will have all the disciples' names (add names on illustration) and for the blank side (the back) the children can draw little faces and bodies for each of the disciples. See example picture. Add lots of bright color and there you have your own little stand-up card decoration.

Craft 2: Following Jesus

(See Student's Book)

Color the illustrations of Jesus and the boy or girl. Cut them out, then glue a cork onto the backs, to help them stand up (1). Take a thin string and make a knot on both ends. With a thumbtack, place the string between the tack and the cork and push in (2). Do this from one cork to the other (from Jesus to the boy or girl). Now you can make Jesus lead the way and the child follows just like how we follow Jesus (3).

Activity Sheets:

(See Coloring & Activity Book)

Color page
What's in the net?

Prayer/Praise idea: Follow the Leader

Children and teachers line up in a row for this prayer time. The teacher begins with a short phrase or sentence prayer along with an action to go with it. For example: "Dear God, thank You for the sun (lifts up hands to make a circle shape). Please give us some rain (makes a gesture for rain falling down)!" All the children repeat the prayer and follow the actions. Each one takes a turn being the "leader" as they think of something to pray for or to thank God for, as they act it out, for the others to follow.

my notes

(Story 40)

Hanging out with Jesus

(Matthew 19:13-15) Lesson topic: KINDNESS

A verse to remember:

"Love is patient. Love is kind. Love never fails." (1 Corinthians 12:4,7)

Tell the story idea:

Write on a big piece of paper the word "Jesus". Cut out plenty of little paper heart shapes. As you're reading the story, every time it talks about Jesus doing something loving and kind, glue a heart onto the word Jesus. Once the story is done, if you still have space on the word, children can think of other loving things that Jesus does to take care of them or show that He loves them, as you continue to glue on more hearts.

Game 1: Letter guess

Each child in turn draws a letter onto the back of the child on their left. That child guesses the letter and says something loving that starts with that letter, a kind word or a kind deed, or someone they love that starts with that letter. If it's too complicated for younger children, instead they can whisper a letter sound to the child on their left.

Discussion:

- Can you tell when someone is doing a sweet thing for you?
- Do you want others to be able to tell when you do something kind for them?
- Then what do you have to do?
- Think about the last time someone did something nice for you? How did it make you feel?
- What activity do you like to do most with your best friend, or you parents or family?
- List all the stories that you can think of where Jesus showed kindness.
- What did Jesus do in this story that showed He was kind?

Game 2: Clothespin tag

Give each child 5 clothespins to pin somewhere onto their clothes. Tell the children that you will all try to think about others during the lesson; what makes them happy, what needs they may have, let them have a turn first, pass the pencils to others, let them answer the question even if you wanted to, give your place in line, let them sit on the comfortable chair, offer to help them, etc.

If at any time during the lesson, a child does one of those kind things for another child, he gets to have one of his clothespins. If someone says something unloving or is greedy or selfish, he loses a clothespin to the person he wasn't nice to.

Discussion:

- How many pegs did you receive?
- How many pegs did you lose?
- Do you always realize when you are saying something loving or unloving?
- Who notices it the most, even when you don't?
- How did it feel when others said or did nice things to you?
- How would your home be, if you did more kind and loving things for your family?
- Who can we go to for more love?

Craft 1: A heart full of love

(See Student's Book)

Place on the table as many magazines as you possibly can. Give each child a heart shape paper, scissors and glue. Children go through the magazines and cut out all the letters (as many as they can find) that spell out the words "I love you!" or just "Love". They glue them onto their papers in order to help remind them of how many ways Jesus shows His love to us, and how many ways there are to show our love for Him and others.

Craft 2: Children of the world door hanger

(See Student's Book)

Children will enjoy creating this little hanger for their room or door handle. Use the illustrations provided for the children to color and cut out. Depending on how much time you have available, they can choose how many kid figures to use. Put together by using string or yarn, taping each figure onto it (1). For the heart, use a colorful ribbon and thread through holes on the top (2). Make a knot and it's ready to hang (3).

Activity Sheets:

(See Coloring & Activity Book)

Color page
What's different?

Prayer/Praise idea:

Hugging Prayer: One child prays for something and then hugs another child in the room who then prays for something else. Continue till each child has had a turn to "hug & pray".

my notes

(Story 41)

Water to Wine Miracle

(John 2:1-11) Lesson topic: CHEERFULNESS

A verse to remember:

"A joyful heart makes a cheerful face." (Proverbs 15:13)

Tell the story idea:

Have a see-through water jug on hand. Bring along some red food coloring or red grape juice to pour into the water as Jesus turns the water to wine.

Game 1: Water to wine Bingo

(See Student's Book)

This is a simple Bingo game to go along with your story lesson. Use the illustrations provided, though you may need to photocopy a few extra depending on the size of your children's group. Cut out the boards and the wine glass cards. To play the game, give each child a Bingo board and place all the wine glass cards into a clay jug or teapot. The teacher calls out questions about the story and whichever child answers first gets to pick a wine glass card from the jug and place it onto one of his water glasses on his board. Or you could give each child a question in turn. If he/she knows the answer, he/she gets a wine glass card. If he doesn't know the answer, he/she doesn't get a card. The first board completed with all the 4 wine glasses is the winner.

A few question ideas: (you can use each one more than once, depending on how many children are playing.)

1. Name one person that Jesus was with at the wedding party? What kind of party was it?
2. What did they serve to drink at the party?
3. Who of Jesus' family was also at the party?
4. What did Mary tell the servants to do?
5. What did Jesus tell the servants to do?
6. Did the servants do exactly as Jesus said?
7. Did the servants grumble and complain when they had to fill the water pots?
8. Why did the servants obey cheerfully, what Jesus asked them to do?
9. What other miracle had Jesus done before this one?
10. What miracle did Jesus do in this story?
11. What did the master say when he tasted the wine?

Discussion:

- What blessing did the servants get for staying cheerful when Jesus asked them to do something?

- What blessings do you receive for staying cheerful?
- How does your face look when your mom or dad ask you do help with something?
- How does your face look when you receive an ice-cream treat?
- What happens when you do a job cheerfully? How do you feel?

Game 2: Two envelopes

(See Student's Book)

You will need two envelopes. On one of them draw a happy face and the other one a sad face. Cut out a slit at the bottom of the sad face envelope. Explain that you have cut a slit so that you will lose and forget about your problems or things that make you sad and miserable. But you will keep safely in your heart and mind all the things that make you happy and cheerful. Now the children can think about the story or come up with other everyday scenarios, as you write them down for them to place into the fitting envelopes. You will find a few examples already written out for you (in student's book), related to today's story, but feel free to encourage the children to come up with some of their own.

Discussion:

- Which envelope would you like to keep and make a part of you?
- What if your heart was an envelope?
- Would you have more cheerful things or complaints in it?

Craft: Water to wine jug wheel

(See Student's Book)

Use the illustration provided. Children color the jug and cut around the circle, as well as the inside of the jug, on the gray lines. Then color the 2nd circle on the inside part, one side light blue and the other red. Now put them together with a paper fastener and children can tell the story of how Jesus turned the water (light blue color) into wine (red color). Glue the verse card in the back to read out together.

Activity Sheets:

(See Coloring & Activity Book)

Color page
Amazing miracle

Prayer/Praise idea:

Pass a cup around with red grape juice as pretend wine and each child takes a sip and then gives praise to God for something that he/she is thankful for.

my notes

(Story 42)

Jesus calms the storm

(Mark 4:35-41) Lesson topic: GENTLENESS

A verse to remember:

"Come and learn from Me, for I am gentle and humble." Matthew 11:28-29

Tell the story idea:

Kids can help act out the story as you're reading it. Use a big blue sheet and half of the kids hold onto the corners. Use a rectangular container or a shoe box as the boat with some Duplo or Lego men inside it, then place it into the middle of the sheet. During the storm the kids pull and lift the sheet to make it as waves that tumble the boat about. Some of the kids (not the ones holding onto the sheet) stand nearby and throw rice or beans onto the sheet as rain, while the rest of the kids can hold out pillows into the air as the puffy dark clouds. When leader reads out "Peace! Be still! The pillows disappear, the rice and beans get picked up and the kids lower the sheet and make it as wrinkle-free as possible.

Game: Journey through the storm

(See Student's Book)

Make your own game board with a large piece of paper or cardstock, or even by drawing on your white board if you don't have anything else. Draw a simple path into the shape of a boat, with squares along the way and number each one. You can even get the children's help to write the numbers. Use the game page provided with all the instruction cards. To play the game, each player places his maker on the START square and rolls a die to determine which number to land on, picking up a card with each roll. First player to the FINISH box wins.

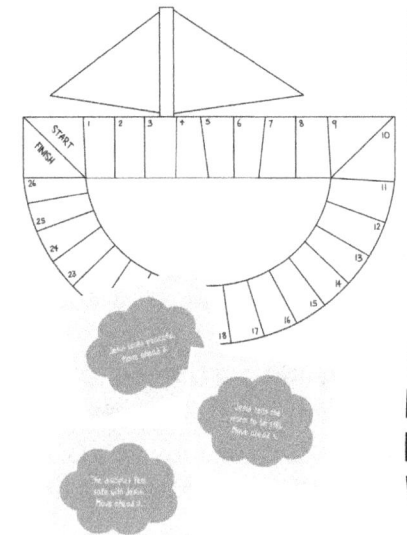

Discussion:

- Do you sometimes find yourselves in the middle of a problem?
- What is your first reaction to the problem?
- What do you do about it? Do you yell for help, or wait quietly till someone is near to ask for help?
- How would you ask Jesus for help, if He were right next to you?
- If you make a mistake or are in trouble, how do you like your parents or teachers to act towards you?
- Do you practice peace and gentleness at home? In what ways? Doing what?

Craft: Storm and Peace puppet

(See Big Bible – little me Craft.)

Give the children their page to color and cut out. Then glue them together, back to back with a popsicle stick in the middle as shown in the example. Now the children can retell the story using their little puppet stick.

Activity Sheets:

(See Coloring & Activity Book)

Color page
Put in order

Prayer/Praise idea:

(See Big Bible – little me Craft.)

Pass out the cards of little everyday scenarios and difficulties to the children. In turn, each child, with their most gentle voice, tells Jesus the problem (reading out the card) and asks for His help and direction.

For example if a child is given the scenario "Your big brother doesn't want to play with you. It seems he's too busy for you." The child could tell Jesus something like: "Jesus, it makes me feel sad when my big brother (or sister) doesn't have time to play with me. Help me to be patient and please work it out for us to spend time together again. Amen." First they can describe how the difficulty or problem makes them feel and then ask Jesus for the answer. It's a good reminder to bring their problems to God, tell Him about them and ask Him for peace and trust as they work through them.

(Story 43)

Doctor Jesus

(Mark 5:21-24, 35-43) Lesson topic: FAITH

A verse to remember:

"A prayer full of faith will save those that are sick and God will make them well." (James 5:15)

Tell the story idea:

Take a girl doll, lay her head on a pillow and cover her with blankets. Prepare a little snack of fruit or crackers to share between the children, when you get to the part of the story where Jesus says to give the girl something to eat.

Game 1: Doctor's bag

Gather a large paper bag and several items from a doctor's toy set or first-aid kit (For example: thermometer, band-aids, a small empty bottle of medicine, a small empty bottle of vitamins, a scale, etc. Children take turns reaching into the bag, feeling an object and guessing what it is. After guessing, the child can display his/her object to the group. Continue the game until the bag is empty.

Discussion:

- In what ways were all the items alike?
- Who uses these items?"
- How does Jesus help sick people?
- What items does He use to help people feel better?
- How do you feel when you're sick?
- How does it feel when someone in your family is sick?
- What do you pray for when you're sick?
- When you pray, do you believe that Jesus can heal you?
- Tell us about a time when you were sick; but you prayed and Jesus helped you get better.
- What is a miracle? (An amazing surprise from God)

Game 2: "My child, get up!"

Choose one child to play the role of Jesus. The remainder of the children pretend to be sick and asleep by lying down on the floor or simply resting their heads on a table top. "Jesus" takes one "sleeping" child by the hand and says, "My child, get up!" That child stands and now gets to play the role of Jesus by taking another sleeping child by the hand. Continue playing until each child has had a turn as Jesus and as the sick child.

my notes

Discussion:

- How do you think the young girl felt when Jesus took her hand and told her to get up?
- How do you think it would feel to hear Jesus call you His child?

Craft: Folded story page

(See Student's Book)

Use the illustration provided for the children to color. Cut on the two black lines until the dotted lines, then fold over on the dotted lines. It should look like the example shown here. Children can then write their own words into the speech bubbles to fit the story, or the teacher can write something on the board for them to copy. Then they can decorate or draw their own story on the front of the flap, as they wish. End by reading the verse together.

Activity Sheets:

(See Coloring & Activity Book)

Color page
Finish the pictures

Prayer/Praise idea:

Thank the Lord for a time that you were sick and Jesus made you well again. Tell him how good it felt to be healed.

my notes

(Story 44)

The Blind can see

(Mark 7:31-37) Lesson topic: ASKING

A verse to remember:

"Ask and it will be given to you. Seek and you will find." (Matthew 7:7)

Tell the story idea:

Bring some blindfolds for the children to try out during your lesson, to see how it must have felt to be totally blind. Have them try walking to the other side of the room or eating from a plate they can't see, or guessing what something is just by feeling it, etc.

Game 1: I spy!

Each child takes a turn to say "I spy with my little eyes something that is blue (or any color chosen)." All the other children try to guess what that object may be. Whoever guesses it correctly gets to "spy" next. Keep going till all the children have had a turn to spy.

Discussion:

- Isn't it a wonderful feeling to be able to see?
- What if you didn't have eyes to see?
- How do you think it would work out for you?
- What do you think would be the most difficult? What would you miss the most?
- Did you know that there are people today who can't see?

Game 2: Learn a rhyme

Here's a little rhyme for the kids to learn together and act out.

Thank You for my eyes so I can see the sky,
(circle fingers around eyes then point to the sky)
And all the beautiful birds as they fly by.
(stretch out your arms and move them up and down)
I can see a rainbow and watch the sun rise.
(make a shape of a rainbow and then scoop your hands up slowly for the rising sun)
Thank You, God, for amazing, wonderful eyes.
(begin with circled fingers on eyes then slowly make the circle shape bigger and bigger)

push down   pull up

Craft: Make the blind man see

(See Student's Book)

Color and cut out the illustration pictures on the gray lines. Include cutting out of the gray mouth and eye area, though the children may need some help for those. You will need a Popsicle stick for each child to glue or tape onto the back of the circle shape. Then glue or tape the little rectangle shape to keep it in place, a shown on the example. Now the children can have fun pushing and pulling up the eyes and mouths as they tell the story.

Activity Sheets:

(See Coloring & Activity Book)

Color page
Make them glad

Prayer/Praise idea:

Fill a bowl with sand (if you don't have any, you could also use rice or beans, lentils, etc.) Along with the sand, hide in some little toys and objects. Blind fold the children, one at a time. That child digs in and hunts for a little object. Once he figures out what it is, he can say a prayer or thank God for something related to that object. A few object idea: Lego man, coin, spoon, pen, hair elastic, button, sponge, toy chair, rock, toy shoes, toy foods, etc.)

my notes

(Story 45)

Lost and Found

(Luke 15:1-7) Lesson topic: BEING RESPONSIVE

A verse to remember:

"Little children, let us not love in word or talk but in deed and in truth." (1 John 3:18)

Tell the story idea:

Use a man from a Lego or Play-mobile set for the shepherd. Use some cotton balls for the sheep and some branches and rocks (to show where the little lost sheep got stuck). Bring along a cloth and a string for the children to use as a headpiece to dress up with as they take turns acting out the shepherd. Try to find a white wooly sweater or coat to put on the pretend sheep.

Game 1: Shepherd and sheep

Children sit on the floor around the room. One child is chosen to be the "shepherd" and has a blindfold on. Another child is chosen to be his sheep. (You can use the shepherd's headpiece and the white fluffy "coat" to dress them up, if you like). They start by being on opposite sides of the room. The shepherd slowly walks around the room trying to find his sheep. The rest of the children help him out by clapping slowly if he is far from his sheep. As soon as he gets a little closer, they clap faster. If he's really close, they clap their fastest. Set a timer for 1 to 2 minutes and then you can change shepherds and sheep so all children get to try out searching for their little lamb.

Discussion:

- How did it feel when you were the shepherd, searching for your little sheep, and you didn't know where to go?
- How did it feel to finally find your sheep?
- While you were looking for your sheep, did you think about your Lego car back at home, or your favorite dessert? Why or why not?
- What do you do when someone is really in need? Maybe they fall down and hurt themselves real badly and there are no adults around. What could you do to help?
- What do you like others to do for you when you need help, for example when you're sick?

Game 2: Find the lost lamb

Give one child a little stuffed animal lamb or toy sheep to hide somewhere in the room. The rest of the children stay seated at the table or on the floor with their eyes covered with their hands. At the "Go!" signal, they go searching for the little lamb.

Whoever finds it first becomes the next one to hide it and the game continues till all the children, who want to, have had a turn to find and hide the lamb.

Discussion:

- What was your favorite part of the game?
- Did you imagine you were the shepherd looking for his lost sheep?
- Do you sometimes lose things around your room or house?
- Who has ever lost a shoe or a sock?
- Was it fun looking for it? Why or why not?
- Did you stop looking for it because it was too difficult?
- Or did you keep looking because you knew you needed it?
- So why didn't the shepherd just stop looking when he didn't find his sheep right away?
- Who never gives up on us, but is always willing to save us and help us?

Craft: A cute lamb figure

(See Student's Book)

Cut out the two oval shapes provided. You will need a box of Q-tips, a bag of cotton and 2 pegs per child. Cut the Q-tips so that you just have the ends. Use 2 ends for the ears, and 3 for the hair (1). Dab white glue onto the places you want to place them then leave to dry. For the body, use cotton wool (2). Add a little ribbon to the top of the hair (for girls) or to the bottom of the head (for boys). Now you're ready to glue the two pegs in place, as the legs (3). Cut out your verse card and peg it to the back. Each child can take their little lamb home and place them on their desk or shelf as a reminder to show love and be responsive to other's needs.

Activity sheets:

(See Coloring & Activity Book)

Color page
Hide and seek

Prayer/Praise idea:

Find a little cuddly stuffed animal for each child, that they can hold and hug tightly as they say their prayer, pretending that they're a shepherd to their little lamb. You can ask the children beforehand, to bring theirs from home. Or you can use one or two that you have on hand and the children can take turns with them. Repeat this prayer together: "Jesus, thank You for being our loving shepherd, our faithful provider and for taking such good care of us. Help us too, to be eager to help when we see someone in need. Help us to respond and do what we can to make others feel better. Amen."

my notes

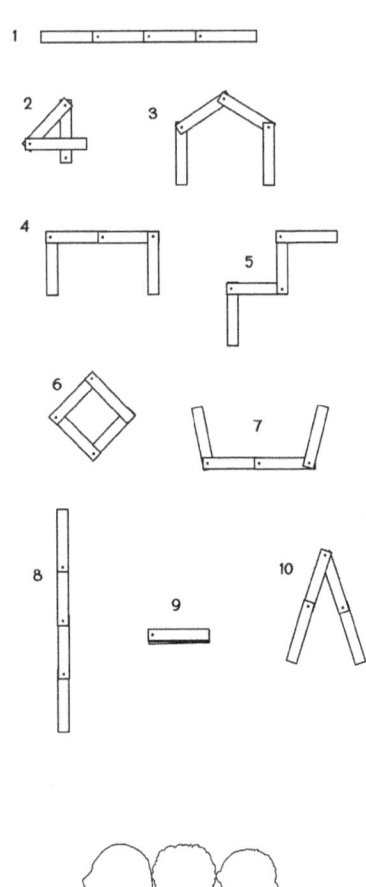

(Story 46)

The Lame Man

(Mark 2:1-12) Lesson topic: FRIENDSHIP

A verse to remember:

"A man that has friends must show himself friendly." (Proverbs 18:24)

Tell the story idea:

Use 4 pieces of cardboard joined together with paper fasteners. See example pictures as you tell the story in a fun unique way. These keywords or phrases may be of help:

1. Man laying on his mat
2. He had 4 friends
3. House where Jesus taught
4. Houses in those days had flat roofs
5. It was too crowded in the house, so took the stairs
6. Made a hole in the roof
7. Tied ropes to the mat to let it down
8. Jesus told the man to get up
9. The man folds his mat
10. And went on his way (legs walking, moving back and forth)

Game: Get up... get up... and walk!

All children sit in a circle on the floor, or on their chairs if you don't have enough floor space. One child is chosen to be "Jesus" and walks around the circle tapping each one's head as he goes by. Each time he taps a head he says "Get up!" He might end up tapping 4 heads and saying "Get up! Get up! Get up! Get up! ... and for the fifth child he says "... and walk!" Instantly that child gets up and tries to catch up with him. "Jesus" runs to the other child's seat. Once he's seated the other child can say thank you and give him a hug. Now it's his/her turn to be "Jesus" and choosing another child to help him/her "get up and walk".

Craft 1: A mobile picture

(See Student's Book)

Color the pictures of Jesus, the man and his friends and then cut them out. Follow example as you tape some yarn or string from each character to the rooftop. As you tell the story, begin with the walking man in the pocket in the back of the roof. Then once Jesus heals the man, switch and put the lame man in the pocket instead, so that you see the walking man with Jesus. Review the verse together before children leave.

Discussion:

- Do you remember a time when Jesus healed you?
  Do you remember of a time when Jesus healed someone else that you knew?
- Have you ever done something to take care of a sick friend or family member? What did you do?
- Who do you like best, to be with you while you are sick?
- Do you miss your friends when you can't play with them?
- What kind deeds could you do for a friend that is sick?

Craft 2: A wreath of friends

Each child is given a colored piece of paper and traces over his/her hand. He/she cuts out the hand shape and then writes or draws something that a friend has helped him/her with, on it. Once all the hands are finished, glue them together into a wreath shape. Add a colorful ribbon to remember how wonderful it is have friends who share a helping hand.

Activity sheets:

(Big Bible – little me color/activity book.)

Color page
Good friends

Prayer/Praise idea: Spin the bottle

Use the 4 pictures provided and place them in the center of your table or floor. Use a water bottle and each child takes a turn to spin the bottle. Whatever picture it lands on (or the closes to one of them) will be for the child to follow as he prays his prayer. Below are a few examples of how to pray:

Laying: Children lay down as they say their prayer. They can also thank God that they don't have to lay down all day like the poor crippled friend did.
Walking: Children walk around as they pray for something.
Leaping: They can pray for something while leaping up and down.
Praising God: Children lift up their arms in the air as they thank God for something.

my notes

(Story 47)

A Boy Shares his Lunch

(John 6:1-14) Lesson topic: SHARING

A verse to remember:

"Be generous and ready to share with others." (1 Timothy 6:18)

Tell the story idea:

Bring along a small basket and fill it with 5 corks (to be used as the bread). Draw some lines or squiggles for the bread patterns. You will also need 2 blue or white bottle tops (to be used as the fish). Draw an eye and mouth. Add some paper fins and a tail, if you like. End your lesson with a tasty snack of smoked fish on mini bread toasts or crackers.

Game 1: Learn a rhyme

Here's a little rhyme that the children can learn together and act out.
I want to be more like Jesus, (point finger up to Jesus)
Be kind and loving too. (give a self hug)
I'll share my smiles; (point to their mouth and smile)
I'll share my toys. (pretend to give away a toy)
I want to please Jesus in all I do. (open arms wide for the "all" word)

Discussion:

- What are some things that you share with others?
- Can you only share physical things, like toys, food or clothes?
- When you think of sharing, who do you think of first?
- Who does most of the sharing when you're with friends? Is it you or your friends, or do you take turns?
- Do you know some people that don't share?
- Why do you think they're that way?
- And how does that make you feel?

Game 2: Change places

Everyone is gathered together in a circle sitting on the floor or on chairs. Leader whispers to each person whether they are a loaf or a fish. One child begins in the middle and has no seat in the circle. He calls out either "loaves" or "fish" and all the children who have the one that he named run to change places with each other. At that time the middle child can try to find a free place. The last one to be seated is now in the middle and it keeps going. To make it more interesting, alter the way they change places. For example: walk, hop, spin, babystep, crawl, gallop, side step, etc.

Craft 1: The boy who shared

(See Student's Book)

Color and cut out the illustration. Fold on the dotted lines and glue small flap over bigger one to make it stand up, as shown on the example. Give each child a sheet of paper to write or draw some of the things that he would like to share with others. They can decorate as they wish before they roll it up and fit it into their little sharing boy figure.

Craft 2: Cardboard basket

(See Student's Book)

Children can color or paint their basket shape, handle, bread and fish. To cut the basket, be sure to cut on the black lines only. The dotted lines are for folding. See example. Glue the corners together and then add the handle. Now give them each some corks and bottle tops and they can have fun creating their own breads and fish out of them, copying the ones that you made for telling the story. Or if you don't have those items on hand, use the bread and fish illustrations provided. Have the children glue in their verse cards to the inside of the basket to read out together before they place their items inside.

Activity Sheets:

(See Coloring & Activity Book)

Color page
Moral of the story

Prayer/Praise idea:

Beforehand, prepare a basket with brown paper bread shapes and blue or gray paper fish shapes. Write out (or draw if your children don't read yet) a prayer request on each bread shape and something to thank God for onto each fish shape. During your prayer time, each child picks out one of each and takes a turn to pray and thank God for those things listed on their papers.

(Story 48)

Stop to Listen

(Luke 10:38-42) Lesson topic: JESUS FIRST

A verse to remember:

"My joy is in listening to God's Word, and I think about it day and night." (Psalm 1:2)

Tell the story idea:

Use two female figurines (from Lego, Playmobile or dolls). Bring a kitchen bowl with a mixing spoon, cutting board and a plastic knife, along with some soft fruit to make into a fruit salad (for Martha to use as you tell the story). Of course the children will be happy to enjoy the snack after the lesson. Bring a pillow and a Bible for Mary to use as she sits and listens to Jesus.

Game: Skit story

Use this little skit to teach a lesson on keeping ourselves centered on what is most important in our lives. A few props: a food paper bag, napkin, straw, packet of ketchup, paper cup with a lid on it (You can get all these items easily from fast-food places).

Do you ever get hungry during church? Sometimes I get so hungry that I just don't think I can make it through the sermon. This was one of those mornings, so I went to MacDonald's and got a hamburger. If you will excuse me, I am going to eat it right now. (Start removing the items from the paper bag one at a time, commenting on each one as you take it out. When you have removed all of the items from the bag, show surprise and concern that something seems to be missing - the hamburger.) Can you imagine that? I got so interested in getting all of these things to go with my hamburger, that I forgot the most important thing. I forgot to get the hamburger!

You probably think I'm pretty foolish to have forgotten the hamburger, after all, that was the most important thing. Well, I am not the only person to ever do something so foolish. That is what our Bible lesson is about this morning. Jesus told Martha, "Martha, Martha, you are worried and troubled about too many things. Only a few things are important, perhaps just one. Mary has chosen that one thing and I will not take it away from her."

Many of us make the same mistake that Martha made. We get so busy working, going to school, playing, or watching television that we often forget the most important thing. We forget to spend time with Jesus! We must be very careful that we don't get so busy doing good things that we leave out the best! After all, Jesus is the most important thing!

Discussion:

- Do you ever forget important things like I did?
- Do you sometimes forget to do the most important thing?
- What is that most important thing?
- How do you remember to spend time with Jesus?

Game 2: Follow the Leader and Listen

Everyone stands in a circle. While the music plays, the leader or a child volunteer does an action of some type of house work; either cooking, stirring, sweeping, cleaning, etc. All the children copy the action. Then it's the next person's turn (in the circle) to do another action, again something related to helping around the home. Everyone copies the action. When the music stops, everyone freezes their action and listens to the leader read out the memory verse. Once done, music begins again and continue playing till all the kids have had a turn to do a different action

Discussion:

- What kinds of jobs do you do at home to help your parents?
- Is it important to do all those things? Why or why not?
- What things do you like to do in your day?
- Do you like to play, go to school, watch TV, eat tasty foods?
- What is something more important than all those things?
- Do your parents take time with God? When do they do this?
- Do you take time with God each day? When do you do it?
- How do you feel after hard work or cleaning and cooking?
- How do you feel after time in God's Word or praying?

Craft: Mary and Martha triangle.

(See Student's Book)

Use the illustration to form a triangle standup card. First, color the illustrations. Then cut each one on the gray lines. For the book, put the two papers together, fold on dotted lines and staple in place. Glue the back of the book onto Mary. For the spoon, cut a slit in Martha's bowl (on little lines) and place spoon inside, moving it around as if mixing. Children can read the verse together and then write a little prayer, asking God to help them find time to spend with Him. Now for the triangle, fold on the dotted lines and add glue to the extra flap to put together, and it's ready to stand up.

Activity sheets:

(See Coloring & Activity Book)

Color page
Guess who

Prayer/Praise idea:

Give a plastic fork to each child and pass the fruit bowl around. For the first round that they poke their fork into the bowl and take a piece of fruit, they can ask God for help in remembering to spend time with Him. The next rounds, they can thank God for something they enjoy doing that includes the Lord.

(Story 49)

A Wounded Traveler

(Luke 10:25-37) Lesson topic: COMPASSION

A verse to remember:

"God is merciful and gracious, full of love and faithfulness. (Psalm 86:15)

Tell the story idea:

(See Student's Book)

Make the little characters beforehand and glue them onto pencils or popsicle sticks to use as visual aids while you tell the story. You can also have different children get up and pretend to be the characters, holding them out from behind a board.

Game 1: Loving feelings or actions

Children sit in a circle on the floor, facing each other. One person is chosen to think of a loving feeling or action. When he/she is ready, he/she passes it on to the next child by acting it out. That second child guesses what it is and says it out loud. If he/she gets it right then it's his turn to act out a loving feeling or do a kind action for the next child in the circle. Finish when all the children have had their turn to guess and act out.

Discussion:

- How did you feel loved today?
- How did you make someone else feel loved?
- Is it always in the things that we say?
- What can be even more important than the things we say?
- What would be some ways to show compassion?

Game 2: Band-aid relay race

You will need lots of wrap around "band-aid" strips (cut out from an old sheet). Divide your group into teams and line up in rows. The first players of each team begin by running to the other side of the room near a chair that has all the strips of band-aids and a dolly per team. They must take a strip and wrap it on the arm or leg or head of the doll and then run back to the team for the next player to do the same. The team who finishes wrapping up their doll first is the winning team.

Discussion:

- How fast were you at running to help the dolly?
- What if it was for real, that someone got hurt?
- Would you think about all the other things you had to finish first?

my notes

- Or would you rush to help as fast as you could, just like you did in this game?
- In what ways can we be quick to help others like that?

Craft: Heart and feet

(See Student's Book)

This little activity shows that if our heart feels loving, our feet will move to action by doing something to help others. If your loving heart feels sad for a sick friend, the feet will go and pay him a visit or go and get him his favorite snack, etc. Use the feet and heart illustrations and have the children color and cut out their own. Give each child 2 long strips of colored paper and teach them how to fold it accordion style. See picture instructions of how to. Glue the ends of the strips together and then one end goes to the middle of the feet and the heart glues on top. Now the children have their own springing feet to show compassion.

Activity sheets:

(See Coloring & Activity Book)

Color page
Follow the path

Prayer/Praise idea:

Give each child a heart shape for them to draw something that they would like God's help with, in showing more love to others. Then take a minute to say a silent prayer to Jesus, asking for help in that area. When each one is done, each child can give an example of when someone was loving and compassionate to them and what they did, as they glue their heart onto a bigger heart to show that God has so much love for us.

my notes

(Story 50)

The Party Boy

(Luke 15:11-32) Lesson topic: FORGIVENESS

A verse to remember:

"Forgive others who have done wrong to you, so that God may forgive you too." (Mark 11:25)

Tell the story idea:

Use 2 Lego or Playmobile people, for the father and the son. Use some pink marshmallows for the pigs, a little bowl or tray from your kitchen for their trough and add some melted chocolate sauce for the mud, that the pigs and boy will get into as you tell the story.

Game: Spin and forgive

Children sit in a circle on the floor or around the table. Use an old plastic bottle to spin around. First player spins and whoever it lands on, they say "I'm sorry if I offended you or hurt you." Child who received the bottle replies: "That's okay. I forgive you!" as a way to practice forgiveness, to help make it easier when it happens for real.

Discussion:

- How did it feel to apologize to someone?
  How did it feel to forgive the person?
- Has there been a time when it was very difficult to say sorry to someone?
- After you apologized, did the person forgive you?
- Pretend you're carrying a huge backpack of heavy rocks (you can try it out if you want). How does it feel?
- Now I'll help you take it off and how does that feel?
- Well, that's a little how forgiveness feels. When we forgive others, we feel a lot lighter and happier.

Craft: The forgiving hug

(See Student's Book)

Use the illustration of the father and the son. Have the children color and cut them out on the gray lines. Turn over the paper and finish drawing inside the folds (the front faces and bodies). Fold on the 2 middle dotted lines to make them standing up facing each other. Then fold the arms over as if they are hugging. You can glue the hands in place or just keep them as folds. Slip the little verse card in between as you are reminded to show love and forgiveness.

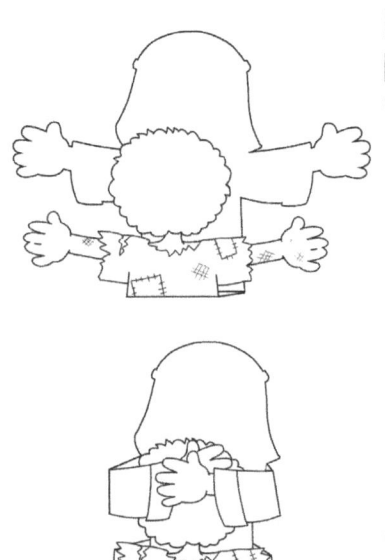

Activity sheets:
(See Coloring & Activity Book)

Color page
Put in order

Prayer/Praise idea: Prayer ball

You will need 5 plastic bottles half filled with water (tightly closed) or 5 empty cans, and a tennis ball (or another ball that size). You will pretend that the ball is like your "prayer". Place the bottles or cans at the end of the table or on the floor by a wall. Each child takes a turn to throw their "prayer ball" aiming at the bottles as he says a prayer (like aiming their prayer on a person or something who is in need). If there are still bottles standing, he prays again for something else, as many times as he needs to knock down all the bottles or cans. Let each child have a turn to pray and knock down the cans.

(Story 51)

A Thankful Return

(Luke 17:11-19) Lesson topic: GRATEFULNESS

A verse to remember:

"Give thanks in all things, for this is obeying and pleasing to God." (1 Thessalonians 5:18)

Tell the story idea:

During the reading, use two child volunteers. One stands in front of the group, while the other has a roll of tissue paper. The child with the roll unrolls the tissue and rolls it around the other child. When he gets tired of doing this, you can ask another child to replace him/her. Continue until the other child is covered head to toe in tissue (pretending to be the man with leprosy). Another child or two can come and help "unravel" him as the story continues with the man being healed. Once he's free he can jump up and down and thank God.

Game: A round of thanks

Sit the children in a large circle with you in the middle. You, the parent or teacher think of an imaginary item that you tell the child you are giving them as you throw him/her a soft ball. For example, a "toy car" or a "bouquet of flowers", etc. As the child reaches to catch the ball, he recites the memory verse: "Give thanks in all things ..." and says a big "Thank you!" Now that child goes to the middle and throws the ball to give something to the next player. Repeat until each child has had a turn to go in the middle and give a gift and give thanks.

Discussion:

- How did it feel to give an imaginary gift?
- How did it feel to give thanks?
- How did it feel to receive a "thank you!"?
- Do you always remember to show your thanks?
- When do you remember the most?
- When do you forget to do it?
- Why do you think you sometimes forget to thank someone?
- Is it difficult when you have to go out of your way to thank someone? Give an example.
- When was the last time someone thanked you for something? And for what? How did it make you feel?

Craft: A gratefulness tree

(See Student's Book)

To help children remember to say thank you throughout the day, use this simple activity as a way to record their thanks.

Give each child their illustrations to color and cut out. (tree trunk, bushes and grass, along with the healed man who returned to thank Jesus). Prepare some green pre-cut leaf shapes to pass out to each child. From now on, whenever the children say "thank you" for something, whether to another child or to the teacher, or to Jesus in prayer, they get to glue a little leaf onto their tree. They can take them home and continue to fill up their tree every time they use their words of thanks. Watch the tree blossom with leaves as the children grow in gratefulness.

Activity sheets:

(See Coloring & Activity Book)

Color page
Hidden message

Prayer/Praise idea: Your name poster

Write out each child's name in big bubble letters. Inside the letters the children write or draw things that make them special and that they want to thank God for. For example: Thank You God that I can run fast, or that I can draw. Thank you God that I'm a big helper to my mom while she cooks, thank You for my long pretty hair, etc.

(Story 52)

A Changed Man

(Luke 19:1-10) Lesson topic: REPENTANCE

A verse to remember:

"If we confess our sins, He will forgive us and show us a better way to live." (1 John 1:9)

Tell the story idea:

(See Student's Book)

Use the illustrations of Zacchaeus to make either into Popsicle stick puppets or glue clothes pegs in the back to peg them onto a house or tree branches, or make them stand up as you glue a roll of toilet paper to the back, etc. to use as you're telling the story.

Game: Musical plates

You will need a paper plate for each player, plus one extra for Zacchaeus. Each person writes out their name in the middle of the place real big. If they know how to write they can also include some characteristics about themselves that they or the other children think of. Include the name Zacchaeus and add some of his characteristics too. For example: short, took people's money, cheater, rich, lonely, no friends, etc. Place all the plates face down in the middle of the floor. Children dance around with some music but as soon as the music stops, they land on a plate. Everyone turns their plate around to see who's name they landed on. Whoever has the Zacchaeus name goes to dinner with Jesus (sits down at the table back at his seat along with his name plate). Keep playing till all the children are sitting with Jesus for dinner.

Discussion:

- Does Jesus know our name?
- Does Jesus know all the things we've done, both good and bad?
- Does He still love us just the same?
- Did he show love to Zacchaeus even though he had been so bad and nobody else liked him?
- What did Zacchaeus do to show that he was sorry?
- Then what did Jesus do to show that He loved him and forgave him?
- What do you do after you've done something wrong?

Craft: Zacchaeus on a tree

(See Student's Book)

You will need an empty toilet paper roll for each child. After children have colored and cut out their leaves and Zacchaeus figure, cut two slits on the top of the roll (1). Slide the leaves in place, onto the roll. Use the strip of paper to place around the roll and glue the ends together, along with Zacchaeus on top (2). Now you can make him slide up and down as you tell the story of him climbing up the tree to see Jesus and then coming back down to have dinner with Him (3). Slide your verse card onto the back of the tree (also into the roll slits), for easy review access.

Activity sheets:

(See Coloring & Activity Book)

Color page
Word search

Prayer/Praise idea:

Have ready an inflated balloon for each child, plus a selection of markers to write on them. Each child writes or draws something that he wants to say sorry to God for. Take a minute of silent prayer for each one to say sorry for the wrong they've done. Then each one throws their balloon up in the air and then catches it again to pop it.

Another alternative, if your children prefer not to pop the balloons because of the loud noises, you could instead bring some helium-filled balloons. The children could write what they are sorry for on a piece of paper and tape it around the balloon's string. Then they could go outside and let go of the balloons as they say sorry to God. Or if you have a high ceiling, they could let their balloons go up to the ceiling out of reach. Explain that when we say sorry to God, He not only forgives us, but also forgets the wrong things we have done and gives us the chance to make a new start.

(Story 53)

Into Jerusalem

(Luke 19:37-38) Lesson topic: ENTHUSIASM

A verse to remember:

"This is the day that the Lord has made. Let's rejoice and be glad about it." (Psalm 118:24)

Tell the story idea:

Get a play donkey and a little man to use for Jesus. Use as many bottle corks or bottle tops or rocks that you have to pretend they are people. Gather some large leaves and cut slits into them and use as all the children raise them and shout "Hosanna to the king!" with them.

Game: Path of praise

Make a "path" by having the children stand in two rows facing each other. Children spread out so the path goes from one end of the room to the other. Talk about the story where Jesus rode into Jerusalem and all the people praised and sang Hosanna! The children take turns to walk through the path as the other children all shout "Hooray! Or Yay, _____ (and the child's name), as they cheer him/her on. They can say whatever encouraging and praiseful words they think of, to make the child walking through the middle feel loved and encouraged. When the child reaches the other end, he rejoins the line and the next child on the starting point walks through. Keep going till all the children have had a turn to walk through the path of praise.

Discussion:

- How did it feel to walk through the middle of the path?
- How did it feel to shout and cheer?
- How do you think Jesus felt when all the people cheered for Him?
- How and when can we praise and show Jesus our thanks?
- How do you show your gratitude or appreciation at home?
- How do you show that you're excited about something?

Craft 1: Jesus on a donkey

(See Student's Book)

Use the illustration for the children to color and cut out. Fold onto the dotted lines. Add glue to the small flap and glue under the bigger flap, so the donkey stands up. Slip the verse card into it before the children leave, so they can go home and practice enthusiasm.

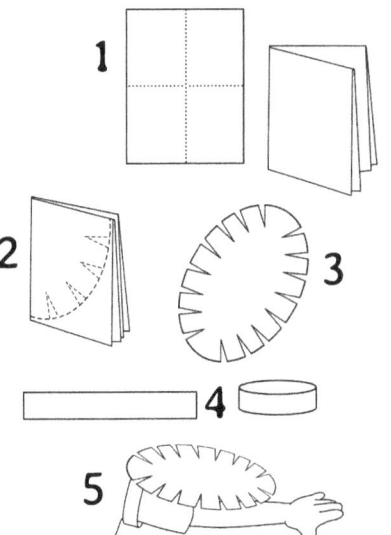

Craft 2: Waving palm branches

Take 2 green A4 size sheets of paper for each child. Make a cross-fold (1). Then on the open side, cut out a curve and cut out 4 little triangle grooves into it (2). Open it up (3) and glue the end onto a strip of paper (4). Tape the paper strip to the top of the kids' arms (5) and then they can flap their arms up and down (as if flying), all the while waving palm branches, as they shout out "Hosanna to the King!"

Activity sheets:

(See Coloring & Activity Book)

Color page
Clippety-Clop

Prayer/Praise idea: "Thumbs up" for God!

Give each child a piece of paper and ask them to trace around their hand and then cut out the hand shape. On each of the four fingers they can write or draw (real small) something that they're thankful to God for. Go around the circle and children thank God for one at a time, in turn. So each child does their pointer finger, then do a whole round of praises with the tall finger, etc. Each time they do, they get to fold the finger over. By the end, all the fingers should be folded over except the thumb. Everyone raises their "hand" in the air and gives a "thumbs up" to God!

(Story 54)

Not just a Snack

(John 13:31-14:14) Lesson topic: COMMUNION

A verse to remember:

Remember Me as you take this time of communion. (Luke 22:19b)

Tell the story idea:

Bring a white table cloth to put over your table or across your floor as the children sit around it. Use some little plastic cups with juice and little crackers or a loaf of bread, to enjoy a snack, as you tell the story.

Game 1: Remember me

For this game you will need different objects, souvenirs and photos. Place them all in the middle of the table for the children to observe. Now explain to them that in turn they will each be able to pick an object and say what that object makes them think of. For example if it's a photo of a grandpa and grandma, they may say that this reminds them of their grandparents. If it's a souvenir from Paris, they may say that this reminds them of their vacation trip to visit Paris, or an object of a baby bottle might make them think of when they were a baby, etc. Once all the children have picked an object and said something, add to the table a piece of bread and a glass of red juice and ask the children what this makes them think of, as you enjoy a piece of bread and a sip of juice together.

Discussion:

- What usually helps us remember things or events? (objects, photos, videos, etc.)
- Did they have all those things in Bible times?
- So Jesus thought of a clever way to remember Him by?
- So what does the bread represent?
- And the wine?
- Is there something that you do just at your home that your friends know about and like and remember you for?

Game 2: COMMUNION round

Children sit in a circle with a big flashcard of the word COMMUNION, to help children spell out the word. Leader begins with calling out the letter C. Next child continues with the letter O and on it goes till the whole word communion has been spelled out. The last child who ends in N says something related to communion, what it means, why we do it, who did it, what it includes, etc.

Then the next child starts again with the letter C, then the next one says O, and then M, and on to play for as long as the children enjoy it. Or you could play another version, where the child sits out everytime he lands on the letter N, until there is only one child left, who is the winner.

Discussion:

- Who knows how to spell the word COMMUNION now?
- And did we get to learn some things about it too?
- Do you feel you know a lot about communion or would you like to learn more?
- Have you ever been to a place where they served communion?
- What did you think about it or how did you feel?

Craft: Jesus and His disciples

(See Student's Book)

Color the pictures, then cut them out. For the table fold over the dotted lines and then add glue to the side flaps to put together. Then glue the 2 pictures of the disciples onto the sides of the table, as shown in the example; the one with 7 characters on the side with 7 plates, 6 characters go to the side with 6 plates. You can glue the little verse card onto the back of the side where Jesus is standing, as a way to be reminded of communion and Jesus' love for us.

Activity sheets:

(See Coloring & Activity Book)

Color page
Find and color

Prayer/Praise idea:

Fill a basket or box full of toys. Each child picks one and thanks the Lord for something that He does for them or related to His love and goodness, that starts with the same letter as the toy they picked.

my notes

(Story 55)

Jesus on the Cross

(Mark 15:1-39) Lesson topic: SALVATION

A verse to remember:

"For God so loved the world that He gave us Jesus His son. If we believe in Him, we will live forever." (John 3:16)

Tell the story idea:

Print and cut out some pictures related to the story (from internet or from an old Bible picture book). Place each one onto a magnet board or metal kitchen tray with some magnets. Children can even come up and help put pieces up as you tell the story. Some other objects you can prepare are: little wooden crosses (1 big and 2 small) made from popsicle sticks or branches, a green sheet or towel as the hill where the crosses stood, a rock to show the tomb where Jesus body was put. You could also use Lego or Playmobile soldiers or knight figures as the guards, and a heart shape to show Jesus' love for us.

Game 1: Washed away

Write "SINS" on the sidewalk with chalk (or on a large paper with a pencil, if you're playing indoors). Say something like: Because we believe in Jesus and what He did for us, we are set free and saved to live with Him forever in Heaven. But our hearts are still guilty and we make mistakes and sin.
Take a big bucket of water outside and each child has a turn to dip a cup in and dump it out onto the word SINS. Let all the children have a turn to wash off the word. Write it over again, if you need to, to give each one a chance. If you're inside, give the children erasers to use instead of the water.

Discussion:

- What happened when you washed (or erased) off the word?
- Who washes away our sins just like the water washed away the guilt?
- What does SIN mean? And why do we sin?
- How did Jesus save us and forgive our sins?

Game 2: Flannelgraph story

(See Student's Book)
Color and cut out the illustrations of the Jesus, heart and children pictures, as you tell the story and give an simple childish explanation of the crucifixion and salvation. Below are a few key words to help you get started, along with the image numbers to use from the illustrations:

1. The children's hearts are sad. (pic. 1,2,3)
2. Jesus knocks on the door of their hearts. (pic. 1,9)
3. Jesus wants to give them His gift of love to make them happy. (pic. 1,8,10)
4. "Jesus, please come into my heart!" the boy and girl pray. (pic. 1,4,5)
5. Jesus is in their heart to stay, forever and ever. (pic. 1,8)
6. Now, the children are happy and full of Jesus' love. (pic. 6,7)

Discussion:

- What are some feelings Jesus may have felt during His crucifixion? (Embarrassment, discouragement, anger, sorrow.)
- How do you think Mary felt? (Sorrowful, helpless, hurt, sad.)
- How do you think God felt to watch His son die? (Pleased with his Son, sorrowful for Jesus' pain, angry at mankind.)
- What do you think about when you think of Jesus dying for our sins?

Craft: Paper plate hill

(See Student's Book)

You will need a paper plate for each child and a cut-up circle the size of the middle of the paper plate. Fold the circle in half and glue the bottom half to the top of the paper plate, turned face down. Children draw and color some grass, bushes, tomb, and a path as shown in example. Cut out the 3 crosses and color in brown, then glue them on the top of the folded circle. Glue the verse card on the side of the plate as a reminder.

Activity sheets:

(See Coloring & Activity Book)

Color page
But why?

Prayer/Praise idea:

Teacher calls out the requests, something to say sorry to God for. All children call out together "We want to say sorry, Lord!" After each request.
For all the times we make You feel sad ... (We want to say sorry, Lord!)
For the times when we lie and cheat ... (Repeat again, etc.)
For the times when we are angry and grumpy ...
For the times when we are rude or naughty ...
For the times when we disobey and do our own thing ...
For the times when we are selfish or unkind ...
For all the wrong things we do ...

my notes

(Story 56)

He is Risen

(Matthew 28:1-10) Lesson topic: EASTER

A verse to remember:

"He is not here. He has risen from the dead just as He said would happen." (Matthew 28:6)

Tell the story idea: A dress-up theater

Bring along some dress-up props to use for the children as you tell the story. For example: a helmet, sword and shield for the guards. A half of a loaf of bread with the inside taken out, for the empty tomb (The inside of the bread could be shared as a snack for the children). A gold crown or hairband, white sheet or dress for the angel. You could cut up some paper angel wings that he can hold in his hands. Pink and red scarves for the women who went to see Jesus' body. For the earthquake, use a green sheet with some wooden blocks as houses and one child can move and shake it all around. The storm could be two children holding a black cloth in front of the window to make it dark. A yellow scarf or pair of socks that one child could use for shooting out lightning rods. The rest of the children could hold up the letters: A, L, I, V, E.

Game 1: Easter egg hunt

(See Student's Book)

Take some colorful plastic Easter egg containers (that you may have saved up after Easter celebrations). If you don't have any, you could use any little plastic boxes or containers or even envelopes. Place the little sentence papers (provided for you in the Craft book) into each one. These sentences all have something related to the story of Easter. Cut them up into 2 or 3 pieces each. For example in one envelope you would have three strips of paper: "Jesus is", "the resurrection", "and the life". You could even add a little mini chocolate as a special treat inside, if you like. Hide the eggs or envelopes around the room and have the children hunt for them. As soon as they find one, they come back to their seats and try to decipher their Easter sentences by putting the words together in order. Once they're done, they can enjoy their yummy treat.

Discussion:

- Did this game remind you of your Easter celebrations?
- Why do you think people use eggs to symbolize Easter? (Beginning of new life with Jesus)
- When do we begin our new life with Jesus? (When we believe in and receive Jesus into our hearts)

Let's celebrate Easter!

Jesus rose from the dead, as He said He would.

Don't delay, share the good news right away!

Hooray! Jesus is alive again!

We love Jesus and He loves us.

Game 2: Rock on a spoon relay

You will need two spoons and two rocks that fit onto the spoon. You can explain that you will be using a rock because it goes along with our story for today: the rock in front of the tomb that moved away when Jesus rose. The children divide into two teams then line up at one end of the room. The first player from each team begins running/walking as fast as they can to the opposite end of the room as they balance their rock on the spoon, and then back again to pass the spoon and rock on to the next player on their team. The first team to make it back to their line is the winner.

Craft 1: Special rock

(See Student's Book)

For this activity, you will need a nice smooth rock per child, some paint and sharpie markers for smaller details and text. The children begin by painting their rock one plain color of their choice. Then they can write a special Easter message on top, surrounded by little decorations of flowers, birds, butterflies or other ideas. Little message suggestions: Jesus is alive! Christ is Risen! Happy Easter! Jesus loves me! Etc.

Craft 2: 3D Picture

(See Student's Book)

Color and cut out all the pictures. Glue a thick piece of cardboard or foam onto the back of the tomb, rock and Jesus. Then follow the example for where to glue them in place; first the tomb, second the rock and lastly Jesus in front. Glue the verse card onto the back as you read it together before leaving class.

Activity sheets:

(See Coloring & Activity Book)

Color page
Wonderful news

Prayer/Praise idea:

Children will love to pray with a "prayer shawl". Any cloth or scarf will do. Depending on how many scraves you have available, will determine how many children do it at a time. The children who have a scarves, cover up their heads and face as they silently say a simple sentence prayer to God. The idea is so that the children are not praying to impress or show off to anyone. Under the scarf he is alone with just God. It will also help him concentrate and make prayer more special. Maybe first you could have one volunteer demonstrate how to do it. The rest of the children can listen to a quiet music until their turn comes around.

112

my notes

(Story 57)

Jesus goes to Heaven

(Luke 24:50-53) Lesson topic: HOPEFULNESS

A verse to remember:

"Our hope is in God's promises, like an anchor, firm and secure." (Hebrews 6:18-19)

Tell the story idea:

Bring a white sheet with you as a robe to dress up as Jesus. Ask some children to stand up and hold up some white pieces of paper cut into the shapes of clouds, as you climb up onto a stool, next onto a chair and then onto the table to show Jesus going up to Heaven.

Game 1: Who's in Heaven?

All the children sit in the middle of the room, on the floor or on their chairs. The leader calls out different Bible story characters or famous people or heroes, fairy tale characters, etc. Tell the children that when they hear a name of someone who they think is in Heaven, they stand up, if they don't think they're in Heaven, they remain seated.

Discussion:

- How can you be certain that someone is in Heaven now or not?
- What does the Bible tell us about Heaven and who will be there?
- Will you be in Heaven one day? How do you know that?
- Do you sometimes think about Heaven?
- What do you know about Heaven?

Game 2: Guess the action

Each child gets a turn to be IT. IT thinks of an action verb of something that Jesus did during His time on earth. (i.e. heal the sick, pray, walk on water etc.) The other children can ask as many questions as they want to try to guess the action. The questions can only be answered with "yes" or "no". Whoever guesses right is the next IT to think of another action word.

(A few ideas of questions you can ask:)
Is it something He did everyday? Did Jesus do it by himself? Did other people see Him do it? Is it something that we do today? Is it something that His disciples did too? Did He use his legs for it? Did He use his mouth? Were people surprised or amazed when He did it? Is it something He did sitting down? Etc.

Discussion:

- After playing this game, what did you learn about Jesus that you didn't know before?
- Did you notice that Jesus did a lot of the same things that we do today?
- What things did only Jesus do and that we can't do?
- Did Jesus' followers do a lot of the same things?
- Does knowing what Jesus did and reading about Him from the Bible help you feel closer to Him? Why?
- How do you think the disciples felt when Jesus had to leave earth and go to heaven?
- Did someone in your family or a friend or a pet die?
- How was that difficult for you?
- What did Jesus say to help make it easier for the disciples not to be so sad?

Craft: Jesus goes up to Heaven

(See Student's Book)

Color and cut out the illustrations. Punch holes on the background picture, at the top and bottom (see example). You will need some string for each of the children (twice the size of the background picture). Tape the middle of the string to the back of Jesus and slip the top of the string inside the top hole, the bottom of the string into the bottom hole. Then turn your picture around and join them together with a knot. Now the children can gently slide Jesus up and down by moving the string up and down in the back of the picture.

Activity sheets:

(See Coloring & Activity Book)

Color page
Odd one out

Prayer/Praise idea:

For fun use a big blue bowl or box, as the heaven and sky. Fill it with lots of little paper cloud shapes, enough for each child. As you call out some prayer requests (friends or loved ones that are sick, those on a trip, special events coming up at your church, etc.), let each child volunteer to take one request and write or draw it onto their paper. Once they're finished, you can hang them on your window. Remind the children to keep that prayer request and pray for it during the week. Then when next week comes along, go over the requests again and see which ones have been answered. Add a shiny sticker to the answered prayers as you rejoice and praise God together.

(Story 58)

Flames of Fire

(Acts 2:1-4) Lesson topic: HOLY SPIRIT

A verse to remember:

"The Holy Spirit will come to you and you will be My witnesses in every part of the world." (Acts 1:8)

Tell the story idea:

Gather some candles as you talk about the flames of fire. (In situations where teachers would rather not light candles with the children, they could make their own paper candles out of card stock.)

Game 1: Holy Spirit Help

(See Student's Book)

Use the simple picture cards provided with some of the ways the Holy Spirit helps us. Cut the cards out and place them in the middle of the table. Each child in turn, picks a card and reads it out loud. Then they give a related example of a difficult situation or a problem they encounter and how God's Holy spirit can help find a solution or work things out. For example, if it's the card "the Holy Spirit helps remind us of things" they could say something like: "When I forget my school lunch, the Holy spirit can help to remind me about it."

Cards and references:
1. The Holy Spirit gives us the words to say. Luke 12:11-13
2. The Holy Spirit gives us peace and trust. John 14:27
3. The Holy Spirit helps remind us of things. John 14:26
4. The Holy Spirit will help teach us. John 14:26
5. The Holy Spirit helps us to tell others about Jesus. Acts 1:8
6. The Holy Spirit helps us to tell the truth. John 16:13
7. We are filled with love through the Holy Spirit. Romans 5:5
8. The Holy Spirit fills us with God's power. Ephesians 3:16
9. God fills us with joy through the Holy Spirit. Romans 15:13

Discussion:

- Can the Holy Spirit help make things easier for us?
- How can we allow God's spirit to help us? (praying and asking for it, being sensitive to listen and follow...)
- When do we make it difficult for God's spirit to help us? (when we forget to ask for help and we choose to follow our own way...)
- When you hear about the Holy Spirit what is the first thing you think of? (a dove, bold witness, etc.)
- Just like the Holy Spirit can help you in your everyday life, how do you think it helped the early Christians?

Game 2: Follow the Holy Spirit

We like to think that we are in control and can do whatever we like, but God knows more than we do; He leads us through His Holy Spirit, if we are sensitive and listen. You will need two pieces of string or yarn and 2 blindfolds. The children line up in two rows. The first child in each row puts on a blindfold and holds on to the end of the strings. At the other end of the strings are the teacher and helper. The child carefully follows the string, not able to see where he is going, but trusting that the string is leading him in the right direction. When he gets to the end, he repeats the words "God's Holy Spirit helps me find my way." Then he takes off his blindfold and gives it to the next player on his team. It might be good for the teacher to explain that it's not a race at all, because what matters is that the Holy Spirit helps each of us to find our own way through life.

Discussion:

- What does this game show and tell us?
- How often do you ask God for His Holy Spirit to help you?
- Do you think we could do better if we did?
- Who remembers what the fruit of the spirit is?

Craft: Tongues of fire crowns

(See Student's Book)

Use one of the illustration provided of the flames, one for each child. They get to color them in red, orange and yellow colors for fire, then cut them out. You will need big strips of paper or cardstock, either red, orange or yellow colors, for each child's crown, large enough to fit around their head. Glue the flame in the front and the verse on the back, as a reminder that they have God's Holy Spirit help if they ask for it, especially when witnessing to others about Him.

Activity sheets:

(See Coloring & Activity Book)

Color page
Be the artist

Prayer/Praise idea: My special helper

(See Student's Book)

Cut out the tongues of fire illustrations and lay them out on the table facing down. Each child picks one and prays something related. If the flame says COURAGE, they could pray something like: "Jesus, please send the Holy Spirit to be my special friend as I learn to have courage and be a faithful witness for You." or if they get the flame of LOVE, "Jesus, please send the Holy Spirit to fill me with lots of love that I can share with others." etc.

116

(Story 59)

The Good News to All

(Acts 18:1-11) Lesson topic: WITNESSING

A verse to remember:
"Go and tell the good news of Jesus to the whole world." (Mark 16:15)

Tell the story idea:
Bring a large globe or world map as you talk about Peter and Paul's travels. Ask the children which countries they've been to, or if they have friends or relatives in other countries. Use an atlas to talk about people in different parts of the world, those who know about Jesus and others who don't, why or why not, etc. You can use little Lego people for Peter and Paul and plenty of dry brown beans or buttons for crowds of people. If you and the children have time, you can make little Lego houses when you talk about Peter and Paul witnessing from house to house.

Game 1: Ball of yarn
All children sitting in a circle. Leader takes a ball of yarn, takes the beginning of it and throws the rest of the ball to another player, as he shouts out some "good news" like God is love! Or Keep smiling! Jesus loves you! Or a simple verse to make the other one happy. Now that player catches the ball of yarn, also holds on to the string and then throws the ball over to another player and does the same thing, sending a happy message of God's love. Continue till everyone is smiling and has gotten the ball of yarn one or two turns. You will end with a huge web of happy news.

Discussion:
- Did the other person smile after you said something?
- How did you feel, receiving the ball and the special message?
- Do you think everyone will want to hear about Jesus? Why or why not?
- If someone doesn't want to hear it, should it stop you from sharing the good news?
- Why did Peter and Paul share the good news with others and why do we do it?

Game 2: Pack my suitcase
Bring a suitcase along, as you act out preparing for a trip around the world. Talk with the kids about where to go, as you look on your map. Then pass out papers for the children to draw objects of what you should pack into your suitcase.

my notes

A few examples could be: lots of Bibles to pass out, tracts with pictures of Jesus or a verse, a flashlight to tell others that Jesus is the light of the world, a passport, hearts to mean love, a smile on your face, a cross to tell people that Jesus died for their sins, a dove picture for the Holy Spirit, etc. Then the children put all their papers inside the suitcase and pretend to go with you to help spread the good news to others around the world, as you go around church to the other groups or the nursery and drop off some of the papers to those you meet.

Craft 1: Paper globe ornaments

(See Student's Book)

Use the strips of paper provided, for the children to color, the land green, the water blue or any other colors they wish. Now cut out each strip and assemble them together with 2 paper fasteners, one at the top, one at the bottom. Color the open Bible that says "good news" on it and tape a piece of string onto the back of it, going down to the brad of the globe. Then glue the verse card on the back of the open book. Color and cut out all the little Bibles and glue them onto some of the strips of the globe, spreading the "good news" around the world.

Craft 2: Good News paper

(See Student's Book)

Gather some old newspapers and give one sheet to each child. Use the illustrations of special "good news" messages for the children to glue anywhere on their paper. Now that's what we call a real news paper! The children can roll them up and take them home.

Activity sheets:

(See Coloring & Activity Book)

Color page
Many ways

Prayer/Praise idea: Around the world prayer

Use a World map or Atlas book for your prayer time today. Each child picks a little marker (you can use different color Lego pieces or buttons, or any board game markers) and places it somewhere on the map or book. Help give them the name of the country they are on. Now they can each have a turn say a little prayer like this: "Dear Jesus, I pray for the people of ___ (say the country name), that more people can learn about You and hear about the good news of Your love. Please help me too, to be a bold witness for You, wherever I go." Keep going till each child has had a turn to pray for his country.

my notes

(Story 60)

John Writes About Heaven

(Revelations 21-22) Lesson topic: HEAVEN

A verse to remember:

"God shows us the path of life. In His presence there is fullness of joy and pleasures forever." (Psalm 16:11)

Tell the story idea:

Before class, gather pictures of things that won't be in heaven (a sick person, someone crying, someone with an angry face, sin, band-aids, war). Also, bring pictures of things that will be in heaven (streets of gold, happiness, Jesus, loved ones, angels, God's Word, tree of life, etc.) Children can help you categorize them.

Game: 4 corners

Use four sheets of different colored papers (light blue, yellow or gold, white and green). Play some music while all the children dance in the middle of the room. As soon as music stops, the children make their way to one of the corners. The leader calls out one of the 4 colors and whoever is at the corner he called, describes something in heaven that is that particular color. For example, if they land on the color blue, they could say: sky, water, lakes, streams, blue jay, etc. Or the color gold: walkways, roofs, crowns, mansions, etc. White: angels wings, robes of light, little lambs, jasmine flowers, etc. Green: trees, grass, leaves, etc.

Discussion:

- What are your favorite colors?
- What is something that you would like to see in heaven?
- When you think of heaven, what is the first thing you think of?
- How long will heaven be for?
- Why is Jesus preparing us this home in heaven?
- What is something you can do to make earth a little more like heaven?

Game 2: Describing Heaven

Make your own sand box, with sand or something similar in texture. Rice or beans will do fine too. Add in some letters from a scrabble or another game that has mini letter blocks. Give each child a spoon and let them go hunting for letters with their spoons, as they try to spell out any of the words that you list on the board (about heaven or from the story).

As soon as a child makes a word with the letters he found, he/she can describe something about heaven using that word.

A few ideas of words you can list on the board:
tall, bright, shiny, golden, sparkly, amazing, magical, special, tasty, mansion, fly, angel, throne, God, friends, family, etc.

Craft: Heaven's gates

(See Student's Book)

Color and cut out the pictures of Jesus in the clouds and Heaven's gates. Fold the gate on the dotted lines. Dab glue onto the two ends of the Jesus illustration, to join with the gate pillars. Now the children can open the gate wide and see Jesus welcoming them in. End by gluing the verse card onto the back of one of the gates.

Activity sheets:

(See Coloring & Activity Book)

Color page
John's visions

Prayer/Praise idea: Roll the die

Put together your die, then children take turns to roll it. Whatever they land on will tell them how to pray for their request.

1. Bible: claim a verse
2. Music note: pick a worship song for everyone to sing the chorus to
3. Repeat picture: everyone repeats your prayer after you
4. Thank you bubble: tell God thank you for something
5. Speech bubble with heart: Pray for someone that needs help.
6. Closed eyes with thought bubble: Everyone closes their eyes and imagines what they would like heaven to be like.

Published by iCharacter Ltd. (Ireland)
Created by Agnes de Bezenac
Illustrated by Agnes de Bezenac
All Bible verses adapted from the KJV.
Copyright. All rights reserved.
www.iCharacter.org

Follow us on Facebook: www.facebook.com/icharacter
See us on YouTube: www.youtube.com/icharactervideos
Follow us on Twitter: www.twitter.com/icharacternews

Copyright © 2016 iCharacter Ltd. All rights reserved. No part of this book may be reproduced in any form or by any electronic or mechanical means, including information storage and retrieval systems, without written permission from the publisher or author, except in the case of a reviewer, who may quote brief passages embodied in critical articles or in a review.

BIG BIBLE, LITTLE ME
VALUES AND VIRTUES FROM THE BIBLE

Don't miss getting your own copy of the book "Big Bible, Little Me". It features 60 charming Bible stories with colorful illustrations, verses and everyday story examples that will help children to apply lessons of value and character, all the while increasing their love and understanding of God's Word.

BIG BIBLE, LITTLE ME
COLORING AND ACTIVITY BOOKS

MORE TITLES AVAILABLE

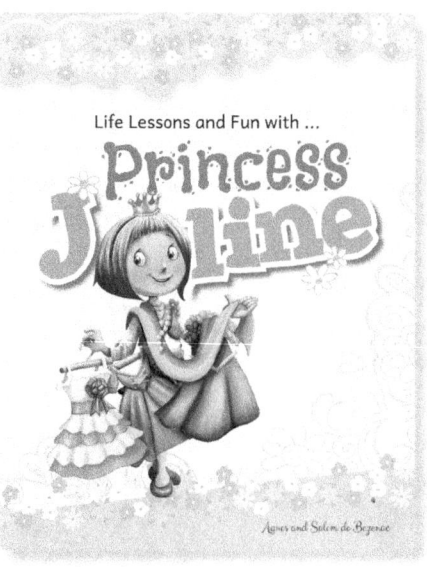

WWW.ICHARACTER.ORG

www.ingramcontent.com/pod-product-compliance
Lightning Source LLC
Chambersburg PA
CBHW080026080526
44586CB00017B/2141